Uneducated

Giacomo Giammatteo

Contents

Did you ever find yourself at a dead—end, not knowing where to go, or which way to turn?

I'm sure Steve Jobs did, or Bill Gates, or Leonardo da Vinci, or Ben Franklin, or any of our presidents who didn't have degrees. But that didn't stop them. They didn't give up. They gathered their wits, made a plan, and persevered. And look where it got them!

Not everyone becomes a billionaire, obviously, but it *is* achievable. Many of the people in this book did it; in fact, 32% of the world's billionaires are people who do not have a degree. You can do it too.

Uneducated

I told all of my kids to go to college. I tell my grandchildren the same. But if I were to meet someone who didn't attend college or who attended but didn't earn a degree, I certainly wouldn't tell them life is over. It may just be beginning.

It might be more difficult to achieve what you want without a degree, but it's been done before, and it *will* be done again.

It's like driving down the road and coming to a toll bridge and the only payment accepted is a degree from an accredited institution. If you have one, great. If you don't have one—don't cry about it. Make a U-turn and find another way to your destination. It might take you longer, but the path is there. Work hard enough, and you'll find it.

##

This is *not* a discourse to dissuade anyone from pursuing a degree. It is *not* a book meant to bash the education system, either. This book is meant to be an example of how someone might be successful *regardless* of circumstances.

Some people go through life with no problems—everything is laid out for them and planned so that nothing goes wrong. But for the rest of us, things usually *do* go wrong. Things *do* happen. And circumstances *must* be taken care of.

To be successful, they say, you *must* obtain an education. But what *is* an education?

What Is an Education, Exactly?

According to dictionary.com, the definition of education is: "the act or process of acquiring general knowledge, developing the powers of reasoning, and preparing oneself for life."

Take a look at that again. Nowhere does it state that the education must be verified, or accounted for, by an institution, or that a person must be educated in a particular discipline. People are so accustomed to judging degrees, especially by the institution who issued them, that they forget what education is about—*learning*.

It doesn't matter *where* you learn something, as long as you learn it. You can learn through reading books (which is basically what you do in college, anyway), or by talking to people (classmates), or by listening (lectures).

When you can explain the difference between learning something at a university and learning the same thing somewhere else, call me. I'd like to know the answer. Learning is learning. It doesn't matter *where* you learn it.

If *you* teach my six-year-old how to recite addition and subtraction figures, or if a teacher at school teaches her, what difference does it make as long as she learns it?

Professors/universities don't hold a monopoly on the secret of how to instruct. Perhaps they *will* reach some people better, but perhaps others learn better in other ways. Who's to say? And it's not something you can control. It's like eating broccoli—you either like it or you don't.

They have schools for just about everything. I once observed a bricklaying class so that I could compare the *professionals* versus the *old-school* types who learned on the job. There wasn't even a contest—the old-school bricklayers demonstrated a far greater skill than the others, even though both had spent the same amount of time on the job (three years).

Perhaps it was because the old-school types were able to choose their educators. They were apprenticed to someone—usually someone they selected—not *assigned* to be taught by someone. It's a subtle but meaningful difference.

But bricklaying isn't engineering, you might say. It's true. Bricklaying *isn't* engineering. It's also not ballet, or carpentry, or language arts, or music, or religion. It's not any of these other disciplines. It's bricklaying. What difference does it make? Learning is learning. No matter what the subject.

Did Galileo have a degree in astronomy? Did he have *any* degree? The answer is *no*. His father sent him to the University of Pisa, but Galileo dropped out. Did this stop him from becoming the "Father of Observational Astronomy" or the "Father of Modern Physics"? Nope.

According to a report by Menachem Wecker in *U.S. News and World Report*, thirty-five of the Fortune 500 CEOs *did not* receive college degrees—that's 7 percent of them. So where did these people receive their education? They got it where everyone gets it—books, other people, and experience. They simply didn't have a piece of paper from an established institution to verify it.

Also, keep in mind that this percentage (7 percent) represents the Fortune 500—some of the largest companies in the United States. If these men and women are savvy enough to run these companies, wouldn't they also be good at running another company? Of course they would, but if job descriptions are to be adhered to, they'd never stand a chance. In thirty years, I have never seen a job description that did not list *some* kind of degree as a requirement.

And why is that? Why do all job descriptions require degrees? Or at least *most* of them? It's simple. We have been trained to think that way. We're taught from the early days of school that *everyone* should go to college. We're led to believe that if you *don't* go to college you're somehow a failure.

Please tell that to the people on this list, or tell the 32 percent of the world's billionaires. I'm sure that news will rattle their cages.

Think about it. Millions of people pay anywhere from thousands to tens of thousands per year for a college education. *Of course* the institutions are going to tell you that you need a degree. And they'll do their best to convince you that the degree needs to be attained right there, at their institution.

Universities are *businesses.* Everything they do is geared toward making a profit. There's nothing wrong with that. Everyone needs to make money, but it does make you wonder about the pressure colleges put on parents *and* kids. And this pressure starts from the day you or your child starts school. It's more like propaganda than anything.

Let me pose a theoretical question. Suppose someone attended a university for almost four years, but something happened during the final two months that prevented them from receiving a degree. Suppose further that this person had been at the top of their class all four years. Who would be more *educated*—the person who excelled but did *not* receive a degree, or the student at the bottom of the class who was awarded a degree?

I'm not saying this happens or that all people without degrees are similar to the one cited in this example, but it *could* be, so why not let other factors come into play? Why not write job specs so that *performance* is the primary screening factor instead of education? The moment you let education factor into a job description, it makes the other requirements secondary.

With something *visual*, it's easy to analyze a person's skills. If you're interviewing a carpenter or bricklayer or ballet dancer, you simply ask for a demonstration. Ask them to get up and *show* you what they can do. Once you observe a performance, it's easy to decide who's better or more suited.

The same applies to any job. You simply have to know what to look for. A candidate might not be able to *show* you their skill during an interview, but their performance in past positions can. All you have to know is what to look for—and how to conduct references.

Now that that's out of the way, let's get on to the real issue—How did so many make it through such a rigid corporate screening process to become successful—in spite of it?

Here is a statistic to chew on:

"Unwelcome news for educators: Net worth of *Forbes* 400 members known to have graduated from college is around $625 million. The average for those who never attended college: $652 million."

—*Forbes*, 1990

Before you say, "Whoa, that was waaaay back in 1990," remember that while 1990 was awhile ago, many of the world's richest people have prospered with the advent of new technologies. Consider Bill Gates (ranked number one and now worth $87 billion) or Larry Ellison or Mark Zuckerberg (both in the top ten now. Back in 1990, they weren't on the list.)

If anything, the years since 1990 have tilted the scales even more, with the rise of people like Steve Jobs, Steve Wozniak, Paul Allen, Steve Ballmer, those mentioned above, and a host of others.

The Successful Ones

(Those Who Were Successful in Spite of Their Situation)

Along with the thirty-five CEOs at the top of the Fortune 500 (or the 32 percent of the world's billionaires), there are many other examples we can look at. I've decided to break them down into a variety of disciplines so that people who are prone to criticize won't say "These are all from the arts, etc."

The fields I chose to use as examples cover a wide spectrum—the arts, business, engineering, fashion, food, inventions, medicine, news/public speaking, politics, science, social media, technology and computing, writing, etc.

Examples can be drawn from all fields. These are but a few.

Special Note

While some may think it's *easy* to make it in nontechnical areas, such as music, movies, real estate, and the like, the facts don't bear that out. In the past thirty years, there have been more billionaires made from technology than from any other field (by non-degreed people).

Perhaps the reason is that more of the new technology companies were made successful by young individuals focused on *getting the job done* or *solving the problem*. Formal education never entered the picture.

It's the way it should be in all industries. If you can do a good job, do it. We don't care about your formal education or lack of it. All we care about is performance.

Consider this short list of technology successes. The founders of *all* of these companies (along with many others) were non-degreed.

- Microsoft
- Apple
- Facebook
- Twitter
- PayPal
- Tumblr
- WordPress
- Oracle (SW)
- Xiaomi
- Dell

You may think it's more imperative that a person has a degree in this industry, where we're dealing with high technology/engineering, but the record speaks for itself.

At one point, the two biggest software companies in the world (Microsoft and Oracle), the three biggest hardware companies, and the largest social media companies were all founded and run by non-degreed people. Is this a coincidence? I think not. These people had the gumption and perseverance to make things work, and they did—despite the odds.

So what *did* these people have that others didn't? They came from different socioeconomic backgrounds, from broken homes and happy homes, and from a variety of ethnic groups. In fact, the only thing I could identify that they had in common was perseverance. Whenever these people failed—and they all failed—they got up and tried again. They never gave up, no matter the odds. That perseverance—combined with a healthy dose of innovation—drove them to ultimate success.

I learned a lot while researching this book, but one thing stuck out—it was obvious to me that optimism (tainted with realism) combined with perseverance and innovation is a key part of success.

- If you don't have enough perseverance, you won't make it through the tough spots.
- If you don't have enough optimism, you won't even try.
- And if you don't have enough realism, you won't be able to make the tough/necessary decisions you're bound to face.
- Innovation provides the tools to move ahead, but the other factors are the drivers to success.

Note
Some of this content was enhanced by articles found on Wikipedia. I used various other sources, like CNW (*Celebrity Net Worth*), and where appropriate, proper attribution/links have been provided.

I understand that some people question—even dispute—the accuracy of *some* information on Wikipedia, but most of the facts I used were checked and verified using other sources. I'm confident that when a fact is cited, it is accurate.

Almost all financial facts and figures dealing with wealth were verified using *Celebrity Net Worth* and *Forbes*. If there was a discrepancy, I typically cited *Forbes*. Other insignificant facts I did not verify but used the information originally cited. For example, if the source mentioned that in 1985, two million computers were shipped, I did not bother verifying that fact if it had no relevance to the topic of discussion. On the other hand, if the source mentioned a company was the largest in the world or number one in a particular field, I did my best to ensure that was accurate.

The Arts
(Acting, Directing, Music, and Movies)

This is the industry I expect the most flak about. People seem to think it's *easy* to make it in music. For example—all you have to do is know how to sing, right?

But that doesn't tell the whole story. You only have to think of the people like MC Hammer, who sold a lot of records and made a lot of money, then lost it in bad investments or spent it on unnecessary items. It's one thing to make money and another to invest and use it wisely.

The people on this list represent those who not only *made* money but then did something productive with that money.

Take Jay Z, for instance. He made a lot of money with his singing, yes, but not $500 million. In addition to his music, his business ventures include a record company, a nightclub, a basketball team, and a clothing line. His money is *not* going to waste. It's growing.

The same can be said for Madonna, P. Diddy, J. Lo, and others—successful people who not only made the money but figured out what to do with it, and all without a university degree.

So how did they do it? Did they surround themselves with the best and brightest? Maybe so. But if they did, that shows an even rarer talent—the ability to recognize your own weakness and *where* to go to resolve it. That's an ability not many people possess. If I had to pick a desirable trait for an aspiring CEO, it would be this one.

Tim Cook is quoted by Macworld (in the December 2012 issue) as saying, "Maybe the most under-appreciated thing about Steve (Jobs) was that he had the courage to change his mind."

Don't get me wrong—he had an unbending will when he felt he was right, but if you showed him differently, he *would* change his mind. Best of all, he had the wherewithal to surround himself with people who knew how to tell him he was wrong and were brave enough to do so.

With all of that said, let's explore the world of music.

Jay Z (Music)

Shawn Carter, who most people know as Jay Z, is a rapper, record producer, and entrepreneur. He may be almost as well-known to those outside the industry as the guy who married Beyonce. And that's fine, as he would probably have never met her if he hadn't been a success already.

He is one of the most financially successful hip-hop artists in America. Several years ago, *Forbes* listed his net worth at almost $500 million. According to CNW, Jay Z is worth $650 million. Combined with Beyonce, his estimated net worth is well over a billion.

Jay Z has sold fifty million records and has been awarded fourteen Grammy Awards for his musical work, as well as other nominations.

Jay Z is consistently ranked as one of the greatest rappers of all time. He was ranked number one by MTV in their list of "The Greatest MCs of All Time" in 2006. Two of his albums, *Reasonable Doubt* (1996) and *The Blueprint* (2001), are considered landmarks in the genre, with both ranked in *Rolling Stone* magazine's list of the five hundred greatest albums of all time.

Jay Z owns a nightclub and was part owner of the NBA's Brooklyn Nets basketball team. He is also cocreator of Rocawear and former CEO of Def Jam Recordings and cofounder of Roc-A-Fella Records.

He holds the record for the most number-one albums by a solo artist on the Billboard—twelve. Jay Z has also had four number ones on the Billboard Hot 100 and is lead artist on one of them.

On December 11, 2009, Jay Z was ranked as the tenth most successful artist of the 2000s by Billboard. He was also ranked as the fifth top-solo male artist and as the fourth top rapper behind Eminem, Nelly, and 50 Cent. He was also ranked eighty-eighth greatest artist of all time by *Rolling Stone*.

Jay Z was born and raised in the tough neighborhood of Bedford-Stuyvesant, but that didn't stop him from succeeding. He was only twenty when he began his career, and he quickly became wildly successful.

In 1988, in Bedford-Stuyvestant, Jay Z had plenty of choices to make regarding his future. He could have been a drug lord, a street thug, or gone into any number of criminal occupations; instead, he made the decision to be a success in the music industry.

I say he made the decision to be a success, and I mean it. He would have had to persevere, as becoming a success was not a given. Plenty of others made that same decision, and he faced a lot of competition.

He must have made the correct choice, because something inside of him rose to the top, and through drive, perseverance, and hard work, he *made it* when others didn't. During an interview with Oprah Winfrey, in the October, 2009 issue of '*O*' *Magazine*, Jay Z said, from his own mouth: "I'm a thinker. I figure things out. I don't have a high level of education, but I'm practical—and I have great instincts."

The music business is tough; the rap business may be tougher. Either way, Jay Z made it a hell of a long way when others didn't.

Oh, and by the way, he never received a formal degree. He has one from the *streets*.

Madonna (Music)

Madonna (born Madonna Louise Ciccone on August 16, 1958) is a singer, songwriter, actress, director, dancer, and entrepreneur. Born in Bay City, Michigan, Madonna moved to New York City in 1977 to pursue a career in modern dance.

She released her debut album in 1983, and followed it with a series of albums that attained immense popularity by pushing the boundaries of lyrical content in mainstream popular music and imagery in her music videos, which became a fixture on MTV.

She has sold more than three hundred million records worldwide and is recognized as the best-selling female recording artist of all time by *Guinness World Records* (no small feat).

Considered to be one of the "25 Most Powerful Women of the Past Century" by *Time* for being an influential figure in contemporary music, she is known for continuously reinventing both her music and her image and for retaining a standard of autonomy within the recording industry.

Many of her songs have hit number one on the record charts, including "Like a Virgin," "Papa Don't Preach," "Into the Groove" "Like a Prayer," "Vogue," "Frozen," "Music," "Hung Up," and "4 Minutes."

Whether you like Madonna or hate her, you must admit she has become a success. She's not only made a lot of money through her music, she's had the wherewithal to do the right things with her money.

To move to NYC by yourself, especially at that age, had to be traumatic, but Madonna succeeded beyond her own, or anyone's, wildest dreams.

She made a career for herself and influenced the lives and careers of countless others—and all from a young woman who dropped out of college. As of this writing, her estimated net worth is $800 million according to CNW—not bad for a girl from Bay City, Michigan.

Steven Spielberg (Movies)

Steven Spielberg (born December 18, 1946) is a film director, screenwriter, producer, and studio entrepreneur. Over that last four-plus decades, Spielberg's films have encompassed an impressive variety of themes and genres. His early science-fiction and adventure films were the forerunners of modern Hollywood blockbuster filmmaking.

In later years, his films addressed social issues, such as the Holocaust, slave trade, war, and terrorism. He is considered one of the most popular and influential filmmakers in the history of cinema. He is also one of the cofounders of DreamWorks movie studio.

In the 1990s, Spielberg won two Academy Awards for best director— one for *Schindler's List* and one for *Saving Private Ryan.*

Three of Spielberg's films—*Jaws* (1975), *E.T. the Extra-Terrestrial* (1982), and *Jurassic Park* (1993)—achieved box office records, each becoming the highest-grossing film made at the time. To date, the unadjusted gross of all Spielberg-directed films exceeds $8.5 billion worldwide.

According to CNW, Spielberg is worth an estimated $3.5 billion.

If you grew up anywhere from the 1970s to the present, it would be tough to say you haven't seen a Spielberg film, no matter what genre you like. If blockbusters such as *Jaws, ET, Raiders of the Lost Ark,* or *Jurassic Park* aren't enough, you can pick from *Saving Private Ryan, Schindler's List*, and dozens of others.

There are few directors with the name recognition of Spielberg. If the theaters announce a new movie by Spielberg, you can bet your last dollar people will flock to see it. And based on his track record, it will probably be damn good.

Robert De Niro (Movies)

Robert De Niro (August 17, 1943) is an actor, director, and producer. His first major film roles were in *Bang the Drum Slowly* and *Mean Streets*, both in 1973. In 1974, he played the unforgettable role of the young Vito Corleone in *The Godfather, Part II*, a role that won him the Academy Award for Best Supporting Actor.

His critically acclaimed, longtime collaborations with director Martin Scorsese began with 1973's *Mean Streets*. The collaboration brought De Niro an Academy Award for Best Actor for his portrayal of Jake LaMotta in the 1980 film *Raging Bull*. He was also nominated for an Academy Award for his roles in Scorsese's *Taxi Driver* (1976) and *Cape Fear* (1991).

In addition, he received nominations for his performance in Michael Cimino's *The Deer Hunter* (1978) and Penny Marshall's *Awakenings* (1990). Also in 1990, his portrayal as Jimmy Conway in Martin Scorsese's *Goodfellas* earned him a BAFTA nomination. No matter how many times you watch that movie, you have to remind yourself that he is just acting.

He has earned four nominations for the Golden Globe Award for Best Actor–Motion Picture Musical or Comedy: *New York, New York* (1977), *Midnight Run* (1988), *Analyze This* (1999), and *Meet the Parents* (2000). De Niro directed *A Bronx Tale* (1993) and *The*

Good Shepherd (2006). He has received numerous accolades for his esteemed career, including the AFI Life Achievement Award and the Golden Globe Cecil B. DeMille Award.

Much like Spielberg, you can't forget De Niro's performances. Young Vito Corleone in *The Godfather II*, Travis Bickle in *Taxi Driver*, Jimmy Conway in *Goodfellas*, or Jake LaMotta in *Raging Bull*—these are only a few of the many unforgettable roles he has played.

In 2012, Bates College awarded De Niro an honorary degree, a long-deserved recognition for his lifetime achievements.

According to reports, De Niro is worth approximately $200 million. His earnings may have started with his acting, but it's his business acumen that has kept him going. He has invested wisely in real estate, opened restaurants, directed films, and co-founded the Tribeca Film Festival in 2002.

Sean Combs (Music)

Sean John Combs (November 4, 1969), also known by his stage names *Puff Daddy, Diddy, and P. Diddy*, is a rapper, record producer, media executive, musician, actor, and entrepreneur. Combs was born in Harlem and grew up in Mount Vernon, New York.

Combs has won three Grammy Awards, two MTV Video Music Awards, and is the producer of MTV's *Making the Band*.

His nonmusic business ventures include the clothing lines Sean John and "Sean by Sean Combs" (for which he earned a Council of

Fashion Designers of America Award), a movie production company, and two restaurants.

According to CNW. P. Diddy is worth an estimated $730 million, making him one of the richest figures in hip-hop. Pretty good for a young man from Harlem/Mount Vernon, New York.

Jennifer Lopez (Music)

Jennifer Lynn Lopez (J. Lo), was born on July 24, 1969. She is an actress, singer, record producer, dancer, television personality, fashion designer, and television producer. According to *Forbes*, she is the most wealthy Latino in Hollywood and the most influential Hispanic entertainer in the United States (according to *People en Español*'s list of "100 Most Influential Hispanics").

She's wisely used her media fame, personality, and popularity to build a fashion line as well as a fragrance she endorses. Outside of her work in the entertainment industry, Lopez advocates human rights, vaccinations, and is a supporter of the Children's Hospital Los Angeles.

Lopez began her career as a dancer on the television comedy program *In Living Color*. She subsequently ventured into acting and gained recognition in the 1995 action-thriller *Money Train*. Lopez's first leading role was in the biographical film *Selena* (1997), in which she earned an ALMA Award for Outstanding Actress.

She earned her second ALMA Award for her performance in the 1998 film *Out of Sight*. She then starred in romantic comedies such as *The Wedding Planner* (2001) and *Maid in Manhattan* (2002).

Lopez had bigger commercial successes with *Shall We Dance?* (2004) and *Monster-in-Law* (2005).

In 1999, Lopez released her debut studio album, *On the 6*, which spawned the number-one hit single, "If You Had My Love." Her second studio album, *J. Lo* (2001), was a commercial success, selling eight million copies worldwide. *J to tha L-O!: The Remixes* (2002) became her second consecutive album to debut at number one on the Billboard 200. Her third and fourth studio albums—*This Is Me . . . Then* (2002) and *Rebirth* (2005)—peaked at number two on the Billboard 200.

In 2007, Lopez released two albums, including her first full Spanish album, *Como Ama una Mujer*, and her fifth English studio album, *Brave*. She won the 2003 American Music Award for Favorite Pop/Rock Female Artist and the 2007 American Music Award for Favorite Latin Artist. To date, Lopez has sold over 25 million albums worldwide. Lopez was ranked twenty-seventh artist of the 2000–10 decade by Billboard.

J. Lo has made a lot of money from her performances in movies and from her music, but again, it's what she did with clothing, perfume, and other ventures that's impressive and puts her at an estimated worth of about $300 million.

Andrew Lloyd Webber (Music/Plays)

Andrew Lloyd Webber (March 22, 1948) is an English composer and impresario in musical theater.

Lloyd Webber has achieved great popular success in musical theater. Several of his musicals have run for more than a decade both in the

West End and on Broadway. He has composed thirteen musicals, a song cycle, a set of variations, two film scores, and a Latin requiem mass. He has also attained a number of honors, including a knighthood in 1992, followed by a peerage from Queen Elizabeth II for his services to music, seven Tony Awards, three Grammy Awards, an Academy Award, fourteen Ivor Novello Awards, seven Olivier Awards, a Golden Globe Award, and the Kennedy Center Honors in 2006.

Several of his songs have been widely recorded and were hits outside of their parent musicals, notably "The Music of the Night" from *Phantom of the Opera*, "I Don't Know How to Love Him" from *Jesus Christ Superstar*, "Don't Cry for Me, Argentina" and "You Must Love Me" from *Evita*, "Any Dream Will Do" from *Joseph and the Amazing Technicolor Dreamcoat*, and "Memory" from *Cats*.

His company, the Really Useful Group, is one of the largest theater operators in London. Producers in several parts of the UK have staged productions, including national tours, of the Lloyd Webber musicals under license from the Really Useful Group. Lloyd Webber is also the president of the leading and most prestigious school for musical theater training in the country, the Arts Educational Schools London, located in Chiswick, in West London.

Webber's estimated worth is $1.2 billion, and his plays and songs are world renowned. Much of his net worth can be attributed to the manner in which he set up the Really Useful Group. He made sure he profited from all aspects of the business, including licensing, record and ticket sales, and all parts of merchandising. So, Webber is not only an amazing musical talent, he is a tremendous businessman as well.

And if you have seen *Phantom of the Opera*, you *know* what a musical talent he is. I believe it holds the record for longest-running Broadway musical.

Business

Ted Turner

Robert Edward "Ted" Turner III (November 19, 1938) is an American media mogul. As a businessman, he is known as founder of CNN, the first twenty-four-hour cable news channel. In addition, he founded WTBS, which pioneered the superstation concept in cable television.

As a philanthropist, he is known for his gift of $1 billion to the United Nations. His gift fostered the creation of the United Nations Foundation, a public charity that has broadened support for the UN. Turner serves as chairman of the United Nations Foundation board of directors.

He took over his father's business when he was twenty-four. At the time, it was worth an estimated $1 million. In 1970, he purchased an Atlanta-based UHF station. It was the beginning of Turner Broadcasting System (TBS). This alone shows Turner's ambition. He could have taken his inheritance and done fine with it (at that time); instead, he risked it all and attempted to build a media empire (which he did), no small feat regardless of who you are. As founder of CNN (Cable News Network), he changed news forever.

Turner is an excellent businessman. He purchased the struggling Atlanta Braves and turned them into a country-wide popular franchise, and his involvement in the WCW (World Champion Wrestling) rekindled interest in the long-forgotten sport and at the same time boosted the ratings of TNT and TBS.

Turner has also devoted his assets to environmental causes. He was, for a while, the largest private landowner in the United States. He used much of his ranch land to repopularize bison meat (for his Ted's Montana Grill chain), amassing the largest herd in the world. He also created the environmental-themed animated series *Captain Planet and the Planeteers*.

Turner attended Brown University, but before receiving a diploma, he was expelled for having a female student in his dormitory room.

He was awarded an honorary BA from Brown University in November 1989, however, when he returned to campus to keynote the National Association of College Broadcasters second annual conference.

CNW estimates Turner's net worth at $2.2 billion (not bad for a kid who was kicked out of college).

Mary Kay Ash

Mary Kay Ash was born in Harris County, Texas. She attended Reagan High School in Houston, and graduated in 1934 but never graduated from college; instead, she married at age seventeen. She had three children, and while her husband was away during WWII, she sold books door-to-door. After the war, she got a divorce and went to work for Stanley Home Products.

Ash retired from Stanley in 1963, when she was passed over for a promotion. The man who received the promotion was a man she had previously trained, and Mary Kay felt she should have gotten the job.

After retirement, she decided to write a book about how to help women in business (and about how a company should be run). The result was a great business plan, and in the summer of 1963, Mary Kay started her cosmetics company with a $5,000 investment.

The original store opened in Dallas, Texas, and the business grew quickly. In 1979, CBS's *60 Minutes* interviewed her, and business then skyrocketed.

Ash seemed to be liked and respected by everyone, and she ran her company the way she would want to be treated. This was a period in US history where women (among others) had a tough time succeeding. One of Mary Kay's goals was to create an environment where women could advance based on merit. According to Mary Kay Cosmetics spokesperson Randall Oxford, more than 150 women earned in excess of $1 million while working at Mary Kay.

As of 2015, the company's sales were approximately $4 billion.

Mary Kay received many awards, some of which include:

- Baylor University's Greatest Female Entrepreneur in American History (2003)
- Horatio Alger Distinguished American Citizen Award (1978)
- Most Outstanding Woman in Business in the 20th Century, Lifetime Television (1999)

- One of America's 25 Most Influential Women, *The World Almanac and Book of Facts* (1985)
- Pathfinder Award, National Association of Women Business Owners (1995)
- PBS and the Wharton School of Business's 25 Most Influential Business Leaders of the Last 25 Years (2004)

No matter how you look at it, Mary Kay achieved a lot. During a period when women had a difficult time in business, Mary Kay not only thrived, she rose from a door-to-door salesperson to running a company that now has sales of more than $4 billion. And she did all of this while remaining a nice person (according to reports).

Henry Ford

Henry Ford was born on July 30, 1863. He was an industrialist, founder of the Ford Motor Company, and sponsor of the development of the assembly line technique of mass production, which was only a gleam in the eye of many a businessman prior to Ford.

Ford did not invent the automobile, but he manufactured the first most people could afford. His launch of the Model-T changed the transportation landscape forever. He became one of the richest and most well-known people in the world. He is credited with "Fordism"—mass production of inexpensive goods coupled with high wages for workers.

He was committed to lowering costs, which led to many innovations, including a franchise system that put dealerships throughout most of North America and in major international cities. Ford left most of his vast wealth to the Ford Foundation but arranged for his family to control the company permanently.

Ford died in 1947, but if he were still alive, he would be worth about $199 billion—that's right, *billion*. And Ford had—you guessed it—no degree.

John D. Rockefeller

John D. Rockefeller was born on July 8, 1839. He was the founder of the Standard Oil Company (now Exxon), which he grew from nothing to one of the largest companies in the world.

Rockefeller started the oil company in 1870, and as the world started relying more and more on gasoline, his wealth grew. He soon became the richest man in the world and was the first American worth more than $1 billion. Adjusting for inflation, he would still be the world's richest person, surpassing Bill Gates by a long shot.

Rockefeller spent the last forty years of his life in retirement. His fortune was mainly used to create the modern systematic approach of targeted philanthropy. He was able to do this through the creation of foundations that had a major effect on medicine, education, and scientific research.

His foundations pioneered the development of medical research and were instrumental in the eradication of hookworm and yellow fever. He is also the founder of both the University of Chicago and Rockefeller University, and funded the establishment of Central Philippine University in the Philippines.

He had four daughters and one son—but no degree.

Wayne Huizenga

Harry Wayne Huizenga was born on December 29, 1939 in Evergreen Park, Illinois. He is an American businessman.

He grew Blockbuster Video, Waste Management, Inc., and AutoNation into successful companies. He is the former owner of the National Football League's Miami Dolphins, the National Hockey League's Florida Panthers, and Major-League Baseball's Miami Marlins.

Starting with a single garbage truck in 1968, he grew Waste Management, Inc. into an entity that would become a Fortune 500 company. Huizenga aggressively purchased independent garbage hauling companies, and by the time he took the company public in 1972, he had acquired 133 small-time haulers. By 1983, he had grown Waste Management into the largest waste disposal company in the United States.

Huizenga repeated his business success with Blockbuster Video, opening a handful of stores in 1987 and becoming the country's leading movie-rental chain by 1994. Eventually, he would also build and acquire several auto dealerships, from which, in 1996, he formed AutoNation, which has become the nation's largest automotive dealer and a Fortune 500 company, and remains his most recent major business venture.

Huizenga has been a five-time recipient of *Financial World* magazine's CEO of the Year award, and was the Ernst & Young 2005 World Entrepreneur of the Year.

In late 2004, he sold his ownership share in a group of hotels that included the Hyatt Pier 66 Hotel and the Radisson Bahia Mar Hotel

& Marina, both in Fort Lauderdale, Florida; the Boca Raton Resort & Club in Boca Raton, Florida; and several others in Naples, Florida, and in Arizona.

It's estimated he's worth $2.6 billion.

Richard Branson

Sir Richard Branson (July 18, 1950) is an English business magnate, best known as founder and chairman of Virgin Group of more than four hundred companies.

His first business venture was a magazine called *Student*, at the age of sixteen. In 1970, he set up an audio-record mail-order business. In 1972, he opened a chain of record stores, Virgin Records, later known as Virgin Megastores. Branson's Virgin brand grew rapidly during the 1980s, as he set up Virgin Atlantic Airways and expanded the Virgin Records music label.

Branson is the fourth richest citizen of the United Kingdom according to the *Forbes* 2011 list of billionaires, with an estimated net worth of US$4.2 billion.

Branson was never awarded a degree.

Engineering and Inventions

Alexander Graham Bell

Alexander Graham Bell was born March 3, 1847. He was an eminent scientist, inventor, engineer, and innovator and is credited with inventing the first practical telephone, among other things.

Bell's father, grandfather, and brother had all been associated with work on elocution and speech, and both his mother and wife were deaf, profoundly influencing Bell's life work. His research on hearing and speech led him to experiment with hearing devices, which eventually culminated in Bell being awarded the first US patent for the telephone in 1876.

A host of other inventions marked Bell's later life, including groundbreaking work in optical telecommunications, hydrofoils, and aeronautics. In 1888, Bell became one of the founding members of the National Geographic Society.

There is no doubt that the phone would have been patented even without Bell; in fact, Elisha Gray tried to submit a patent for the phone shortly (hours, even) after Bell, but Bell was first.

But each invention has to be credited to someone, and let's face it,

Bell was ahead of the game. His invention was the impetus behind the original Ma Bell and the current communications system.

Bell has been described as one of the most influential figures in human history, yet he possessed no degree.

Thomas Alva Edison

Thomas Alva Edison (February 11, 1847– October 18, 1931) was an American inventor, scientist, and businessman who developed many devices that greatly influenced life around the world, including the phonograph, the motion-picture camera, and a long-lasting, practical electric lightbulb.

Dubbed "The Wizard of Menlo Park" (Menlo Park is now Edison, New Jersey) by a newspaper reporter, he was one of the first inventors to apply the principles of mass production and large-scale teamwork to the process of invention and therefore is often credited with the creation of the first industrial research laboratory.

Edison is considered one of the most prolific inventors in history, holding 1,093 US patents, as well as many patents in the United Kingdom, France, and Germany. He is credited with numerous inventions that contributed to mass communication and, in particular, telecommunications. These included a stock ticker, a mechanical vote recorder, a battery for an electric car, electrical power, recorded music, and motion pictures.

His advanced work in these fields was an outgrowth of his early career as a telegraph operator. Edison originated the concept and implementation of electric-power generation and its distribution to homes, businesses, and factories—a crucial development of the modern industrialized world. His first power station was on Manhattan Island, New York.

While it's true that Edison's team *discovered* many of his inventions, he had the business savvy to *do* something with those inventions. There are many inventions that sit in people's laboratories gathering dust. Edison didn't let that happen.

This is the true genius of Edison. To invent something is great, but to figure out what to do with it another thing entirely. And, as you may have surmised, he did not possess a university certificate or college degree.

Nikola Tesla

Nikola Tesla's legacy is alive and well in almost all media outlets. He did not receive much recognition during his lifetime, but he *is* getting it now, featuring his life prominently in movies like *The Prestige,* with Hugh Jackman, and having Tesla Motors named after him.

While he was alive, he was in a long-standing feud with Thomas Edison (whom he worked for earlier) regarding the effectiveness of alternating current (AC) over direct current (DC). Edison ended up the victor, and went on to earn the fame, while Tesla faded into the background (at least temporarily). Although the debate over whether AC or DC is better continues in many circles.

Unlike many of the people on our list, Tesla did not amass great wealth or even great fame (at least in his lifetime), but his work did have a lasting impact on the future of technology.

It also goes to show that even though Tesla possessed no degree (he dropped out of Graz University), he was far from *uneducated.*

Tesla Motors (based in Silicon Valley and named after Nikola Tesla) manufactures electric cars and electric storage systems.

Architecture

Frank Lloyd Wright

Frank Lloyd Wright was born on June 8, 1867 and died on April 9, 1959. He was an architect, interior designer, writer, and educator who designed more than one thousand structures, five hundred and thirty-two of which were completed. A recent search of his name in Architecture Digest drew 208 results, with dozens of houses for sale well above the $500, 000 mark.

Wright believed in designing structures that were in harmony with humanity and its environment, a philosophy he called organic architecture. This philosophy was best exemplified in his design for Fallingwater (1935), a residential structure which has been called "the best all-time work of American architecture."

Wright was a leader of the Prairie School movement of architecture and developed the concept of the Usonian home, his unique vision for urban planning in the United States. His work includes original and innovative examples of many different building types, including offices, churches, schools, skyscrapers, hotels, and museums.

Wright also designed many of the interior elements of his buildings, such as furniture and stained-glass. He authored twenty books and many articles and was a popular lecturer in the United States and in Europe.

Wright was recognized in 1991 by the American Institute of Architects as "the greatest American architect of all time."

I don't know what Wright was worth, but it doesn't matter. I doubt he was penniless, and his recognition and accomplishments are everlasting.

Fashion

Ralph Lauren

Ralph Lauren (October 14, 1939) is a fashion designer, philanthropist, and business executive. He is best known for the Ralph Lauren Corporation, a clothing company and global, multibillion-dollar enterprise.

Lauren stepped down as chief executive officer of the company in September 2015 but remains its executive chairman and chief creative officer.

As of January 2015, *Forbes* estimates his wealth at $8 billion, which makes Ralph Lauren the 155th richest person in the world.

Lauren was born in the Bronx, in New York City, and attended day school before eventually graduating from DeWitt Clinton High School in 1957. He was known by his classmates for selling ties to his fellow students. In a later interview about his early ambitions, he referred to his Clinton yearbook, where it states under his picture that he wanted to be a millionaire.

Through hard work and an abundance of perseverance, he far surpassed that goal.

Food

Rachael Ray

Rachael Domenica Ray is America's most-loved chef, though she never had proper culinary training and never went to a cookery college. She's also an author and TV personality.

Rachael has several cooking shows on the Food Network, a talk show on NBC, several *New York Times* best-selling cookbooks, and her own magazine. She got her start teaching cooking classes to customers at Cowan & Lobel, a gourmet market in Albany, New York. The classes taught customers how to cook meals in thirty minutes or less. In 2008, Forbes.com ranked Rachael seventy-sixth in the Celebrity 100, reporting her earnings at $18 million a year.

Her estimated net worth is $60 million.

News

Walter Cronkite

Walter Cronkite, Jr. (born 1916) was an American journalist and radio and television news broadcaster who became preeminent among the outstanding group of correspondents and commentators developed by CBS News after World War II. Walter Cronkite was born in St. Joseph, Missouri, and, while he was still a youngster, the family moved to Texas.

In 1933, he entered the University of Texas at Austin and took a part-time job with the *Houston Post*. This set him on a professional career that led him to abandon college after two years to serve as a general reporter for the *Post*, a radio announcer in Kansas City, and a sportscaster in Oklahoma City.

After that, his principal employer for several years was United Press International (UPI), for whom he covered World War II in Europe (1941–45) and served as chief correspondent at the Nuremburg War Crimes Trials (1945–46) and in Moscow (1946–48).

To this point, Cronkite was largely unknown to the public. In 1950 he joined CBS News, where two years later he narrated for *You Are There*, a television program in which major historical events were recreated. In 1954 he became narrator of *The Twentieth Century*, a monumental television documentary that established Cronkite's reputation with the public.

When Cronkite assumed the duties of anchor and editor for the *CBS Evening News* in 1962, NBC's *Huntley-Brinkley Report* dominated viewer ratings. Gradually the CBS broadcasts gained ground on the renowned team at NBC, which broke up in 1970. From then until his retirement, Cronkite's program was consistently the most popular television news broadcast.

Although the evening news was his main platform, Cronkite maintained his prominence as narrator and correspondent on network specials, including space shots, major documentaries, and extensive interviews with world figures such as Presidents Truman, Eisenhower, and Johnson. After his retirement, he continued this role in addition to the intermittent series *Walter Cronkite's Universe.*

Among Cronkite's strengths were his believability, accuracy, and impartiality. He was quite diligent about not becoming part of the story he was reporting. Yet there were memorable instances when he failed to remain completely detached, like with his obvious emotional reaction when announcing the death of President John Kennedy in 1963; his characterization on the eve of the 1968 Democratic convention, of the site as a concentration camp; his broadcast pronouncement in 1968, upon returning from Vietnam, that he doubted US policy for that region could prevail; and his undeniable enthusiasm when Neil Armstrong became the first person on the moon in 1969.

Despite his philosophic disclaimer, Cronkite sometimes influenced the news, as in his televised interview with Anwar Sadat, which led that Egyptian leader to visit Israel, and Israeli Prime Minister Menachem Begin to reciprocate. Inadvertently, Cronkite was a news topic in 1976 when John Anderson, running as an independent presidential candidate, mentioned Cronkite as his likely running mate.

The exceptions notwithstanding, Cronkite raised television news broadcasting to a level of professionalism lauded around the world. His credentials as a newspaperman and war correspondent, along with his unwillingness to deviate from a hard news format, demonstrated that acceptance and popularity in television news need not rest on superficiality.

The depth of respect for his work was reflected in the numerous awards he received: the Peabody for Radio and Television Award and the William Allen White Award for Journalistic Merit, as well as the Emmy. In 1981, during his final three months on the *CBS Evening News*, Cronkite received eleven major awards, including the Presidential Medal of Freedom.

In 1985 he became the second newsman, after Edward R. Murrow, to be selected for the Television Hall of Fame. At his retirement, Cronkite was the most commonly mentioned person on the "dream list" for lecturers at conventions, clubs, and college campuses.

You can read more here: Biography.

Politics

Abraham Lincoln

The man has his image on the five-dollar bill and on Mount Rushmore for God's sake. What more can you want?

Abraham Lincoln is best known as the sixteenth president of the United States, but he was also the man who led this country during the Civil War, one of the most tumultuous times in our country's history. During those few years (1861–1865), he also managed to preserve the Union, abolish slavery, strengthen the federal government, and modernize the economy—all without ever going to college; in fact, according to a 2002 article in the NY Times, Lincoln accumulated less than one year of formal education.

This is the man who many claim to have been the most influential and most successful (politically speaking) of the US presidents, and yet, he had no degree.

Although some people would argue that all recent presidents (since Truman) have had degrees, and that a degree is necessary to understand modern technology, I only need to point to people like Jobs, Gates, and Zuckerberg to make my point.

Benjamin Franklin

Benjamin Franklin was an accomplished inventor, scientist, writer, philosopher, statesman, diplomat, and signer of the Declaration of Independence. He never graduated from college but instead received his education from life experience.

Franklin's father sent Benjamin to the Boston Latin School at age eight. His father hoped Ben would become a preacher. When it became obvious Ben would not pursue that career, his father had him transferred to a school (George Brownell's English school for writing and arithmetic) that focused on math and writing.

Franklin stayed at George Brownell's school until he was ten, when family finances dictated that he stop his formal education in order to take up a post at his father's candle-making store.

At age twelve, Benjamin took an interest in the business of printing and assumed an apprenticeship in the printing office of his brother James.

There is no additional evidence of formal schooling. A review of his history clearly shows that where Benjamin Franklin went to school is not as important as his contribution to history and the knowledge he brought to bear as a Founding Father.

Franklin may have been described as a Renaissance man. He was knowledgeable about, and interested in, a broad array of subjects, and he drew on that knowledge to solve complex problems.

Franklin became a successful newspaper editor and printer in Philadelphia, the leading city in the colonies, and published the

Pennsylvania Gazette at the age of twenty-three. He became wealthy publishing both the *Gazette* and *Poor Richard's Almanack.*

He pioneered and was the first president of the Academy and College of Philadelphia, which opened in 175. That institution later became the University of Pennsylvania. He organized and was the first secretary of the American Philosophical Society and elected president in 1769.

Not willing to stick with success in just one field, Franklin became the inventor of a number of things, including the glass harmonica, the Franklin stove, bifocal glasses, and a flexible urinary catheter. And who can forget his experimentation with electricity and subsequent invention of the lightning rod? No wonder he is listed as a Renaissance man.

He was also the first US ambassador to France.

You can read more here: Biography

Social Media

Jan Koum

Jan Koum is cofounder and CEO of the mobile messaging service WhatsApp.

Koum grew up outside Kiev, Ukraine, and moved to California with his mother when he was sixteen.

Koum dropped out of San Jose State University, where he was studying math and computer science, and took a job at Yahoo, where he worked for nine years in systems security and infrastructure engineering.

He got the idea for WhatsApp in 2009 as a way to display status messages next to friends' names in address books. It eventually became a mobile messaging system with 450 million monthly users. In February 2014, Facebook acquired WhatsApp for a reported $19 billion.

Not bad to go from a San Jose State drop-out to billionaire in just a few short years.

Mark Zuckerberg

Mark Zuckerberg was born on May 14, 1984, and yes, you read that right—1984, as in 80 plus 4. He's that young. When Facebook, the company he founded in 2004, went public (2012), he became the world's youngest self-made billionaire.

At the time of this writing, his estimated net worth was approximately $42 billion, and the social media company he founded had about 1.5 billion members.

Since 2010, Zuckerberg has been named among the one hundred wealthiest and most influential people in the world as *Time* magazine's Person of the Year. In 2010, a fictionalized account of Zuckerberg's life was made into a film, *The Social Network*.

From his early years, Zuckerberg showed promise as a programmer, and by the time he began taking classes at Harvard, (according to an article by *New Yorker* magazine in 2010) Zuckerberg had already achieved a "reputation as a programming prodigy."

Zuckerberg dropped out of Harvard in his sophomore year and moved to Palo Alto, California, with Dustin Moskovitz, Facebook cofounder, and some other friends. They leased a small house that served as an office. Over the summer, Zuckerberg met Peter Thiel (a venture capitalist), who invested in the company.

They got their first genuine office in mid 2004. According to Zuckerberg, the group planned to return to Harvard but eventually decided to remain in California. They had already turned down offers by major corporations looking to buy the company.

On July 21, 2010, Zuckerberg reported that the company reached the 500 million-user mark. When asked whether Facebook could earn more income from advertising as a result of its phenomenal growth, he explained (according to a Wired.com article in 2010), "I guess we could. . . . If you look at how much of our page is taken up with ads compared to the average search query. The average for us is a little less than 10 percent of the pages and the average for search is about 20 percent taken up with ads. . . . That's the simplest thing we could do. But we aren't like that. We make enough money. Right, I mean, we are keeping things running; we are growing at the rate we want to."

In 2010, Steven Levy, who authored the 1984 book *Hackers: Heroes of the Computer Revolution*, wrote that Zuckerberg "clearly thinks of himself as a hacker." Zuckerberg said that "it's OK to break things . . . to make them better."

Facebook instituted "hackathons," held every six to eight weeks, where participants had one night to conceive of and complete a project. The company provided music, food, and beer at the hackathons, and many Facebook staff members, including Zuckerberg, regularly attended. "The idea is that you can build something really good in a night," Zuckerberg told Levy (according to the book, *Hackers: Heroes of the Computer Revolution*). "And that's part of the personality of Facebook now. . . . It's definitely very core to my personality."

Vanity Fair magazine named Zuckerberg number one on its 2010 list of the Top 100 "most influential people of the Information Age." Zuckerberg ranked number twenty-three on the *Vanity Fair* 100 list in 2009. In 2010, Zuckerberg was chosen as number sixteen in New Statesman's annual survey of the world's fifty most influential figures.

In a 2011 interview with PBS after the death of Steve Jobs, Zuckerberg said that Jobs had advised him on how to create a management team at Facebook that was "focused on building as high quality and good things as you are."

Love it or hate it, Zuckerberg has succeeded in creating something the world can't seem to do without. I know some who are on Facebook hours per day. Everything they do is recorded there via pictures, videos, and posts.

As of this writing, Zuckerberg's net worth is listed as $42.5 billion, placing him in the top-ten list of the world's wealthiest people.

Evan Williams

Cofounder and former CEO of Twitter, Evan Williams attended the University of Nebraska for a year and a half before leaving school to pursue a freelance career in information systems. He worked for Hewlett-Packard and Intel before he and partner Meg Hourihan launched the blogging platform Blogger, which was acquired by Google in 2003.

Williams and Hourihan also cofounded Pyra Labs, a project-management software company. Blogger was a spin-off of a note-taking feature and was one of the first Web applications enabling the creation and management of weblogs. Williams invented the term "blogger" and was also instrumental in the popularization of the term "blog." Pyra survived the departure of Hourihan and other employees, and was eventually acquired by Google on February 13, 2003.

In 2003, Williams was named to the *MIT Technology Review*'s TR100 as one of the top one hundred innovators in the world under the age of thirty-five. In 2004, he was named one of *PC Magazine*'s People of the Year, along with Hourihan and Paul Bausch, for their work on Blogger.

Later, he and Noah Glass founded the podcast company Odeo, where he hired Biz Stone and Jack Dorsey. The four men—*none of whom hold college degrees*—eventually brainstormed the microblogging platform Twitter in 2006, which went public in November 2013.

Without Williams and his band of hooligans, would 350 million users per month have anywhere to chat?

Technology

Paul Allen

Born in 1954 in Seattle, Washington, Paul Allen met fellow Lakeside School student and computer enthusiast Bill Gates when Allen was just fourteen and Gates twelve. Less than a decade later, in 1975, the two college dropouts founded Microsoft with the intention of designing software for the new wave of personal computers.

By the time Allen arranged for Microsoft to buy an operating system called Q-DOS for $50,000, the company was already supplying software for emerging companies such as Apple and Commodore. Gates and Allen reinvented Q-DOS as MS-DOS and installed it as the operating system for IBM's PC offering, which dominated the market after its release in 1981.

From these humble beginnings, Gates and Allen propelled Microsoft to be one of the premier companies in the world, and the company, in turn, took the two entrepreneurs to the status of billionaire.

Allen, who is billionaire cofounder of Microsoft, founder of Xiant software, owner of the Seattle Seahawks and Portland Trail Blazers, dropped out of the University of Washington to work for Honeywell. A year later he convinced Bill Gates to drop out of Harvard and move to Albuquerque, New Mexico, to start up Microsoft. Again, say what you will about Paul Allen, but he was a huge part of Microsoft's success. Who's to say what would have happened if he hadn't convinced Gates to drop out of Harvard? Would Microsoft even exist? We'll never know. (And if it did exist, would it be the same company it is today? I doubt it.)

Michael Dell

Michael Dell (February 23, 1965) is a business magnate and author. He is known as the founder and CEO of Dell, Inc., one of the world's leading sellers of personal computers (PCs). He is ranked as the forty-first richest person in the world on the 2012 *Forbes* Billionaires list, with a net worth of $15.9 billion as of March 2012.

In 2011, his 243.35 million shares of Dell stock were worth $3.5 billion, giving him 12 percent ownership in the company. His remaining wealth of roughly $10 billion is invested in other companies and managed by a firm called MSD Capital (Dell's initials).

Dell attended Memorial High School in Houston, Texas, selling subscriptions to the *Houston Post* during the summer. While making cold calls, Dell observed that newlyweds and people moving into new homes were the most likely to buy a subscription, so he targeted this demographic by collecting names from marriage and mortgage applications. Dell earned $18,000 that year, exceeding the annual income of his history and economics teacher.

In January 1984, Dell banked on his conviction that the potential cost savings of a manufacturer selling PCs directly had enormous advantages over those selling them via conventional, indirect retail. In January 1984, Dell registered his company as PC's Limited.

In 1992, at the age of twenty-seven, Dell became the youngest CEO to have his company ranked in *Fortune* magazine's list of the top five hundred corporations.

In 1996, Dell started selling computers over the Web, the same year his company launched its first servers. Before long, Dell Inc. was reporting close to $1 million in sales per day through dell.com.

In the first quarter of 2001, Dell Inc. reached a world market share of 12.8 percent, passing Compaq to become the world's largest PC maker. This metric marked the first time the rankings had shifted over the previous seven years. The company's combined shipments of desktops, notebooks, and servers grew 34.3 percent worldwide and 30.7 percent in the United States at a time when competitors' sales were shrinking.

In 1998, Dell founded MSD Capital L.P. to manage his and his family's investments. Investment activities included publicly traded securities, private equity activities, and real estate. The firm currently employs eighty people and has offices in New York, Santa Monica, and London. Dell is not involved in its day-to-day operations.

On March 4, 2004, Dell stepped down as CEO of Dell Inc. but stayed on as chairman of the board, while Kevin Rollins, then-president and COO, became president and CEO. On January 31, 2007, Dell returned as CEO at the request of the board, succeeding Rollins.

Accolades for Dell include Entrepreneur of the Year (at age twenty-four) from *Inc.* magazine; Top CEO in American Business from *Worth* magazine; and CEO of the Year from *Financial World*, *Industry Week*, and *Chief Executive* magazines.

Dell serves on the Foundation Board of the World Economic Forum, the executive committee of the International Business Council, the U.S. Business Council, and the governing board of the Indian School of Business in Hyderabad, India. He previously served as a member of the U.S. President's Council of Advisors on Science and Technology.

Dell's success did not come from an advanced degree, or any degree, for that matter; it came from determination and hard work combined with ingenuity and good business sense.

Bill Gates

Business magnate and philanthropist Bill Gates III was born October 28, 1955. Gates is the former chief executive and current chairman of Microsoft, the world's largest personal-computer software company, which he cofounded with Paul Allen after the two dropped out of college.

He is consistently ranked among the world's wealthiest people and was the wealthiest overall from 1995 to 2009, excluding 2008, when he was ranked third. In 2011, he was the wealthiest American and the second wealthiest person in the world.

During his career at Microsoft, Gates held the positions of CEO and chief software architect, and he remains the largest individual shareholder, with 6.4 percent of the common stock. He has also authored and coauthored several books.

Gates is one of the best-known entrepreneurs of the personal computer revolution. In the later stages of his career, Gates has pursued a number of philanthropic endeavors, donating large amounts of money to various charitable organizations and scientific research programs through the Bill & Melinda Gates Foundation, established in 2000.

Early Life

Gates graduated from Lakeside School in 1973. He scored 1590 out of 1600 on the SAT and enrolled at Harvard College in the autumn of 1973. While at Harvard, he met Steve Ballmer, who later succeeded Gates as CEO of Microsoft.

Gates did not have a definite study plan while at Harvard and spent a lot of time using the school's computers. He remained in contact with Paul Allen and joined his friend at Honeywell during the summer of 1974.

The following year saw the release of the MITS Altair 8800 based on the Intel 8080 CPU. Gates and Allen saw this as the opportunity to start their own computer software company. Gates dropped out of Harvard at this time. He had talked this decision over with his parents, who were supportive once they realized how serious Gates was about starting a company.

After reading the January 1975 issue of *Popular Electronics*, which detailed the Altair 8800, Gates contacted Micro Instrumentation and Telemetry Systems (MITS), the creators of the new microcomputer, to inform them that he and others were working on a BASIC interpreter for the platform.

In reality, Gates and Allen did not have an Altair and had not written code for it; they merely wanted to gauge MITS's interest. MITS president Ed Roberts agreed to meet them for a demo, and over the course of a few weeks, they developed an Altair emulator that ran on a minicomputer, and then the BASIC interpreter. The demonstration, held at MITS's offices in Albuquerque, New Mexico, resulted in a deal with MITS to distribute the interpreter as Altair BASIC.

Paul Allen was hired on at MITS, and Gates took a leave of absence from Harvard to work with Allen at MITS in November 1975. They named their partnership "Micro-Soft" and had their first office located in Albuquerque. Within a year, the hyphen was dropped, and on November 26, 1976, the trade name "Microsoft" was registered with the Office of the Secretary of the State of New Mexico.

Gates never returned to Harvard to complete his studies.

Microsoft's BASIC was popular with computer hobbyists, but Gates discovered that a pre-market copy had leaked into the community and was being widely copied and distributed. In February 1976, Gates wrote "Open Letter to Hobbyists" in the MITS newsletter saying that MITS could not continue to produce, distribute, and maintain high-quality software without payment.

Although this letter was unpopular with many computer hobbyists, Gates persisted in his belief that software developers should be able to demand payment. Microsoft became independent of MITS in late 1976 and continued to develop programming language software for various systems. The company moved from Albuquerque to its new home in Bellevue, Washington, on January 1, 1979.

During Microsoft's early years, all employees had broad responsibility for the company's business. Gates oversaw the business details but continued to write code as well. In the first five years, Gates personally reviewed every line of code the company shipped and often rewrote parts of it as he saw fit.

IBM approached Microsoft in July 1980 regarding its upcoming personal computer, the IBM PC. The computer company first proposed that Microsoft write the BASIC interpreter. When IBM's representatives mentioned that they needed an operating system, Gates referred them to Digital Research (DRI), makers of the widely used CP/M operating system.

IBM's discussions with Digital Research went poorly, and they were unable to reach a licensing agreement. IBM representative Jack Sams mentioned the licensing difficulties during a subsequent meeting with Gates and told him to acquire an acceptable operating system. A few weeks later Gates proposed using 86-DOS (QDOS), an operating system similar to CP/M, which Tim Paterson of Seattle Computer Products (SCP) had made for hardware similar to the PC.

Microsoft made a deal with SCP to become the exclusive licensing agent, and later full owner, of 86-DOS. After adapting the operating system for the PC, Microsoft delivered it to IBM as PC-DOS in exchange for a one-time fee of $50,000.

Gates did not offer to transfer the copyright for the operating system because he believed other hardware vendors would clone IBM's system. They did, and the sales of MS-DOS made Microsoft a major player in the industry. Despite IBM's name being on the operating system, the press quickly identified Microsoft's influence on the new computer, with *PC Magazine* asking Gates if he was "The Man Behind The Machine?"

Gates oversaw Microsoft's restructuring on June 25, 1981, which reincorporated the company in Washington State and made him president of Microsoft and chairman of the board.

Windows

Microsoft launched its first retail version of Microsoft Windows on November 20, 1985, and in August, the company struck a deal with IBM to develop a separate operating system called OS/2. Although the two companies successfully developed the first version of the new system, mounting creative differences caused the partnership to deteriorate. It ended in 1991, when Gates led Microsoft in developing a version of OS/2 independent of IBM.

Management Style

From Microsoft's founding in 1975 to 2006, Gates had primary responsibility for the company's product strategy. He aggressively broadened its range of products, and wherever Microsoft achieved a dominant position, he vigorously defended it. During this time he earned a reputation for being distant with others; as early as 1981, an industry executive publicly complained that "Gates is notorious for not being reachable by phone and for not returning phone calls."

Another executive recalled that after he showed Gates a video game and defeated him thirty-five of thirty-seven times, when they met again a month later, Gates "won or tied every game. He had studied the game until he solved it. That is a competitor." (This was according to Fred Thorlin, who was at the time a director for Atari.)

As an executive, Gates met regularly with Microsoft's senior and program managers. Firsthand accounts of these meetings describe him as verbally combative, berating managers for perceived deficiencies in their business strategies or for proposals that placed the company's long-term interests at risk.

Gates's role at Microsoft for most of its history was primarily managerial and executive. However, he was an active software developer in the early years, particularly on the company's programming language products.

He has not officially been on a development team since working on the TRS–80 Model 100 but wrote code as late as 1989, which shipped in the company's products. On June 15, 2006, Gates announced that he would transition out of his day-to-day role over the next two years to dedicate more time to philanthropy. He put Ray Ozzie in charge of day-to-day management and Craig Mundie in charge of long-term product strategy.

In April 2010, Gates was invited to speak at the Massachusetts Institute of Technology, where he asked the students to take on the hard problems of the world in their futures.

Personal Life
In 1999, his wealth briefly surpassed $101 billion, causing the media to call Gates a "centibillionaire." Despite his wealth and extensive business travel, Gates flew coach until 1997, when he bought a private jet.

Gates began to appreciate the expectations others had of him when public opinion mounted suggesting that he could give more of his wealth to charity. Gates studied the work of Andrew Carnegie and John D. Rockefeller, and in 1994 sold some of his Microsoft stock to create the William H. Gates Foundation.

In 2000, Gates and his wife combined three family foundations into one to create the charitable Bill & Melinda Gates Foundation, the largest transparently operated charitable foundation in the world. Unlike other major charitable organizations, such as the Wellcome Trust, the foundation allows benefactors access to information regarding how the organization's money is being spent.

The generosity and extensive philanthropy of David Rockefeller has been credited as a major influence on Gates. He and his father met with Rockefeller several times and modeled their giving, in part, on the Rockefeller family's philanthropic focus, namely those global problems that are ignored by governments and other organizations. As of 2007, Bill and Melinda Gates were the second-most generous philanthropists in America, having given over $28 billion to charity. They plan to eventually give 95 percent of their wealth to charity. Gates's wife urged people to take a lesson from the philanthropic efforts of the Salwen family, who sold their home and gave away half of its value, as detailed in *The Power of Half*.

Recognition

Time magazine named Gates one of one hundred people who most influenced the twentieth century, as well as one of the one hundred most influential people in 2004, 2005, and 2006. *Time* also collectively named Gates, his wife Melinda, and U2's lead singer Bono as the 2005 Person of the Year for their humanitarian efforts.

In 1994, he was honored as the twentieth Distinguished Fellow of the British Computer Society. Gates has received honorary doctorates from Nyenrode Business Universiteit, Breukelen, the Netherlands, in 2000; the Royal Institute of Technology, Stockholm, Sweden, in 2002; Waseda University, Tokyo, Japan, in 2005; Tsinghua University, Beijing, China, in April 2007; Harvard University in June 2007; the Karolinska Institutet, Stockholm, Sweden, in January 2008; and Cambridge University in June 2009.

He was also made an honorary trustee of Peking University in 2007 and an honorary Knight Commander of the Order of the British Empire (KBE) by Queen Elizabeth II in 2005. In addition, entomologists even named the Bill Gates flower fly, Eristalis gatesi, in his honor.

In November 2006, he and his wife were awarded the Order of the Aztec Eagle for their philanthropic work around the world in the areas of health and education, particularly in Mexico, specifically in the program "Un país de lectores."

In October 2009, it was announced that Gates would be awarded the 2010 Bower Award for Business Leadership of the Franklin Institute for his achievements in business and philanthropic work. In 2010 he was honored with the Silver Buffalo Award by the Boy Scouts of America, its highest award for adults, for his service to youth.

In 2011, Bill Gates was ranked as the fifth most powerful person in the world, according to *Forbes*.

Investments

- Cascade Investments LLC, a private investment and holding company, incorporated in United States, is controlled by Bill Gates, and is headquartered in the city of Kirkland, Washington.
- bgC3, a new think-tank company founded by Bill Gates.
- Corbis, a digital image licensing and rights services company.
- TerraPower, a nuclear reactor design company.

As of the time of this writing, Gates is listed as the richest man in the world, at $87 billion.

Steve Jobs

I realize this section on Jobs is lengthy, but I felt it was necessary. Whether it results from my fascination with the man or his impact on technology, I don't know, but I recommend reading it. Jobs was a doer, and what he did has affected us all.

Steve Jobs was born Steven Paul Jobs on February 24, 1955, in San Francisco, California. He died in Palo Alto on October 5, 2011, when only fifty-six-years old. He was the cofounder of Apple Computer (Apple) and later served as its CEO and chairman. He cofounded Apple in 1976, with his long-time friend, Steve Wozniak.

Industries Disrupted

Steve Jobs was the *great disruptor*. By that I mean he brought revolutionary change to more industries than anyone in the history of business. It's tough to change/affect an entire industry, but Jobs did it more than anyone.

When Apple was founded as a partnership in 1976, Ronald Wayne received 10 percent of the stock but relinquished it for $800 less than two weeks later. A 10 percent stake in Apple today is worth about $50 billion. (Wayne should have kept his stock.) On a much smaller scale, I sold five thousand shares of Apple stock in the early 90s at $4.50 per share. You can bet I've let a few curse words fly since then.

As far as industries disrupted, let's look at a few:

- Cameras (iPhone)
- Computer animation (Pixar)
- Computer input (mouse)
- Mobile phones (iPhone)
- Music (iPod and iTunes)
- Personal computing (Mac)
- Tablet computers (iPad)

While the list above is alphabetical, we'll try to tackle them chronologically.

Personal Computing
When Jobs and Wozniak founded Apple in 1976, a revolution was born. It signified the real birth of personal computing and marked the first time the average homeowner could afford a computer. Even more so, Apple emphasized the reasons *why* a homeowner might *want* to own one.

The original Apple and subsequent models were a start, but the development of the Macintosh, along with its revolutionary GUI (graphical user interface) and input device (mouse) sealed the deal. For the first time, ordinary people could use a computer without having to know code. All that was required was to be able to point and click—oh, and drag icons across the screen.

Computer Input Devices

As far as computer input goes, no, Jobs did *not* invent the mouse; however, he is the one responsible for bringing the idea to the computing world. Jobs first saw the mouse at Xerox's research facility in Palo Alto. The original device used three buttons, was cumbersome, and cost $300.

Jobs was fascinated with the possibilities, however, and he took the idea to Dean Hovey, an industrial designer. He explained that he needed the device to be user-friendly and that it had to cost less than fifteen dollars. Hovey cut out two of the buttons, fixed the design, and found success. As a result, the modern-day mouse was born.

Computer Animation

In 1986, Jobs acquired the computer graphics division of Lucasfilm, which was spun off as Pixar. He was credited in *Toy Story* (1995) as an executive producer and served as CEO and majority shareholder until Disney's purchase of Pixar in 2006.

Pixar single-handedly upended manual animation, which had been the mainstay for decades. As a result of their success, Disney's acquisition of Pixar made Jobs the largest shareholder in Disney Films. In the years he ran Pixar, Jobs revolutionized the computer animation business.

Music (and the iTunes Store)

In the late 1990s, Apple purchased NeXT, and Jobs came with them. He took over as interim CEO of Apple, and later that role became permanent. In his position as interim CEO, Jobs revamped Apple's product line, streamlining it to avoid confusion.

One of Jobs's best moves was the introduction of the iPod. Music players appealed to everyone—PC and Mac users—and with the iPod, Jobs gave everyone a chance to see for themselves how user-friendly Mac products were. In the process, he disrupted the industry with a business (along with the iTunes Store) no one saw coming.

Jobs had the foresight to make downloading music easy and inexpensive, with his insistence on $.99 downloads. Not a bad idea, since Apple has now sold more than 25 *billion* songs—and, yes, that's billion, not million.

Mobile Phones (and the App Store)

When Jobs announced his intention to build mobile phones, a Motorola executive laughed and said Jobs didn't know what he was getting into.

He should have saved his laughter and bought Apple stock instead. The iPhone has gone on to become one of the world's most successful products and has propelled Apple to the top of the corporate world in the process.

Besides setting record sales, the iPhone has forever changed the way smartphones are designed and the way the mobile Web is accessed. In the process, Apple has sold hundreds of millions of iPhones in the past five years.

App Store

It's not like apps weren't sold before the iPhone, but try to remember what it was like. Apps had to be sought out on the Web, paid for with PayPal or a credit card, and then downloaded to your computer. Afterward, they had to be synced with your mobile device using a third-party app on your desktop.

Now all you have to do is search for the app you want on the App Store and hit download. With your credit card securely stored on your iTunes account, you're set. Apple has sold billions of dollars of apps in a short time, as evidenced by the downloads of more than 40 *billion* apps. And apps for the iPhone have already begun to overtake traditional handheld gaming devices. I expect more innovation in the near future.

Digital Cameras

Digital cameras have been around for a long time, but now they come free with every smartphone (iPhone, Android, etc.). Even the convenience of the first digital cameras (ones without film) wasn't enough. People didn't like lugging them around. There was no place to put them. They were bulky and cumbersome.

That all changed with the advent of the iPhone and the host of smartphones that followed in its footsteps. Now every smartphone has a digital camera built into it, and usually it's a damn good camera. Best of all, it's quick, handy, has plenty of storage space (assuming you're frugal), and typically a cloud option for keeping your memories safe (iCloud, Dropbox, and many others).

And it's not just digital cameras you get with your smartphone; most have digital video, and at high quality. I can't tell the difference between the photos or video I take with my new iPhone versus a $400 digital stand-alone camera (and I wouldn't spend $400 for a stand-alone).

It's had a drastic effect on the sales of digital cameras (not single-lens reflex cameras (SLRs) but compact digital cameras). Sales have been down about 25 percent, and I can't see it doing anything but continuing the slide from there. SLR sales, on the other hand, may very well continue to increase, as they are geared toward the professional photographer.

Tablets

Tablets have been around for a while, but it wasn't until the iPad was introduced in 2010, with the App Store, that the market really took off. iPads sales have dominated the tablet market, and though most competitor's product has been labeled "the iPad killer" by damn near every pundit out there, none have succeeded in dethroning Apple's market position.

Apple, which was once known solely as a computer company, now offers products in music, phones, desktops, laptops, tablets, music players, watches, and a host of accessories, including the recently acquired Beats headphones. The iTunes store has sold billions of songs and the App Store has sold billions of dollars worth of software products.

And all this was driven by a man who never finished his degree.

Jobs may best known for his ability to see the needs of the consumer long before they themselves know what they need. He is also renowned for his *persuasive* ability, which came to be known as the "reality distortion field," especially when referring to his product-launch speeches.

In keeping with Jobs's philosophy of minimalist design and in anticipating the needs of the customer, Apple was the first company to abandon the floppy disc and CD drive. These actions received a huge negative reaction at first, but in hindsight, you might ask yourself, "What on God's earth would I do with a floppy disc?" In a few years' time, I'm sure we'll be saying the same thing about the CD drive.

Apple's Early Years

In the late 1970s, Apple cofounder Steve Wozniak engineered one of the first commercially successful lines of personal computers, the Apple II series. Jobs was among the first to see the commercial potential of Xerox PARC's mouse-driven graphical user interface, which led to the creation of the Apple Lisa and, one year later, the Macintosh. He also played a role in introducing the LaserWriter, one of the first widely available laser printers.

Jobs left Apple in 1985 following a power struggle with John Sculley. When Apple's board of directors sided with Sculley, Jobs went on and became founder of NeXt Computer. In 1986, he bought the graphics division of Lucasfilm and spun it off as Pixar.

Pixar was extremely successful, producing such classics as *Toy Story*, and upending the computer animation industry in the process. Jobs served as CEO until Disney bought the company in 2006, making Jobs the largest Disney shareholder and putting several billion dollars in Jobs's pockets.

Jobs returned to Apple in 1996—after Apple's decision to purchase NeXt Computer—and served as interim CEO. The NeXt platform became the basis for the Mac OS X. Jobs is credited with bringing Apple from near bankruptcy to extreme profitability in just two short years. In 2014 it was listed as the most valuable company in the world (based on stock value). It has been called by many the greatest corporate turnaround in history. As of this writing, Apple has more than $200 billion in cash—that's more than most countries.

To give you an idea of how much cash that is, here are a few statistics. It's...

- more than all the gold in Fort Knox
- more than five times the *combined* value of *all* the Major League Baseball teams.
- about $600 for *each* person in the United States.

Many more examples could be given, but I think you get the point—that's a *lot* of money,

Jobs will undoubtedly be known as a visionary and perhaps as the father of the digital revolution, but most will probably remember him as a person with an unbending will and a burning desire to make things perfect.

Early Life and Education

It's strange how things work and how we often end up where we're supposed to be. When Jobs was just a small child, his adopted father taught him how to take apart and repair electronics, which instilled in Jobs a love and passion for that kind of work. Who knows? If not for the adoption, Jobs might never have met Wozniak, and Apple Computer would have never come to be.

Jobs enrolled at Reed College, in Portland, Oregon, but never completed his degree—he dropped out after six months. He eventually joined Wozniak, and after a few sporadic sales ventures, they settled in on building "computers."

Wozniak was the technical guru behind the electronic design, and Jobs was the marketing mastermind. Some have said Jobs got more credit than he deserved as he never designed anything, but he had a far greater gift. Like the ancient Romans, Jobs had the ability to analyze something and determine what was wrong and what needed to be done to make it right. He would then use his undeniably persuasive personality, combined with his unbending will, to get it done.

Pixar and Disney

In 1986, Jobs bought the Graphics Group (later renamed Pixar) from Lucasfilm's computer graphics division for $10 million, $5 million of which was given to the company as capital. As mentioned previously, the first film produced by the partnership, *Toy Story* (1995), brought fame and critical acclaim to the studio.

Over the next fifteen years, under John Lasseter, Pixar's creative chief, the company produced numerous box-office hits:

A Bug's Life (1998)
Toy Story 2 (1999)
Monsters, Inc. (2001)
Finding Nemo (2003)
The Incredibles (2004)
Cars (2006)
Ratatouille (2007)

WALL-E (2008)

Up (2009)

Toy Story 3 (2010)

Finding *Nemo, The Incredibles, Ratatouille, WALL-E, Up, and Toy Story 3* each received the Academy Award for Best Animated Feature, an award introduced in 2001.

In the years 2003 and 2004, as Pixar's contract with Disney was running out, Jobs and Disney chief executive Michael Eisner tried but failed to negotiate a new partnership, and in early 2004, Jobs announced that Pixar would seek a new partner to distribute its films after its contract with Disney expired.

In October 2005, Bob Iger replaced Eisner at Disney and quickly worked to patch relations with Jobs and Pixar. On January 24, 2006, Jobs and Iger announced that Disney had agreed to purchase Pixar in an all-stock transaction worth $7.4 billion. When the deal closed, Jobs joined the Walt Disney Company's board of directors and became its largest single shareholder, with approximately 7 percent of the company's stock.

Jobs's holdings in Disney far exceeded those of Eisner, who holds 1.7 percent, and of Disney family member Roy E. Disney, who until his 2009 death held about 1 percent of the company's stock and whose criticisms of Eisner—especially that he soured Disney's relationship with Pixar —accelerated Eisner's ousting.

Upon Jobs's death, his shares in Disney were transferred to the Steven P. Jobs trust led by Laurene Jobs.

Return to Apple

In 1996, Apple purchased NeXT for $427 million, bringing Jobs back to the company he'd cofounded two decades earlier.

One year later, Gil Amelio was removed as CEO, and in July 1997, Jobs was named interim chief executive officer.

In an effort to stop bleeding out cash, Jobs terminated a number of projects, such as Newton, Cyberdog, and OpenDoc. He also changed the licensing program for Macintosh clones, making it too costly for manufacturers to continue making machines. With the purchase of NeXT, much of that company's technology found its way into Apple products, most notably NeXTSTEP, which evolved into Mac OS X. Soon, Apple was making major headway in the consumer electronics and music distribution business.

On June 29, 2007, Apple entered the cellular phone business with the introduction of the multi-touch display iPhone, which also included the features of an iPod and, with its own mobile browser, revolutionized the mobile browsing scene. While stimulating innovation, Jobs also reminded his employees that "real artists ship."

Wealth

Although Jobs earned a salary of only one dollar a year as CEO of Apple, he held 5.426 million Apple shares worth $2.1 billion, as well as 138 million shares in Disney worth $4.4 billion. *Forbes* estimated his net wealth at $8.3 billion, making him the forty-second-wealthiest American in 2010.

Management style

Jobs was a demanding perfectionist who aspired to position his businesses and their products at the forefront of the information technology industry through foresight and trendsetting, at least in innovation and style. He summed up that self-concept at the end of his keynote speech at the Macworld Conference and Expo in January 2007 by quoting ice hockey player Wayne Gretzky:

"There's an old Wayne Gretzky quote that I love. 'I skate to where the puck is going to be, not where it has been.' And we've always tried to do that at Apple. Since the very very beginning. And we always will." This was recited at the beginning of a video tribute to Jobs produced by Apple after his death. If you look at what Jobs and Apple have accomplished, it is obviously something that Jobs believed in, and something he succeeded in establishing in the minds of Apple's employees.

Ever a stickler for quality, Jobs once famously quipped: "Be a yardstick of quality. Some people aren't used to an environment where excellence is expected." This was repeated in a 2009 article by BusinessBrief regarding Jobs's Twelve Rules of Success.

Tim Cook (Apple CEO) once said about Jobs (and was quoted by Macworld in the December 2012 issue), "Maybe the most under-appreciated thing about Steve was that he had the courage to change his mind."

Reality Distortion Field (RDF)

Apple's Bud Tribble coined the term "reality distortion field" in 1981, in describing Jobs's charisma and its effect on the developers working on the Macintosh project. Tribble claimed the term came from Star Trek. Since then it's been used to refer to many people's perceptions of Jobs's keynote speeches.

The RDF was said by Andy Hertzfeld to be Jobs's ability to convince himself and others to believe almost anything, using a mix of charm, charisma, bravado, hyperbole, marketing, appeasement, and persistence.

Though it was at times the subject of criticism, Jobs's so-called reality distortion field was also recognized as creating a sense that the impossible was possible. Once the term became widely known, it was often used in the technology press to describe Jobs's sway over the public, particularly regarding new product announcements.

Perhaps the most important aspect of this talent was Jobs's ability to persuade people that something could be achieved when they believed otherwise.

Inventions and designs

Although Jobs wasn't an engineer, he is listed as either primary inventor or co-inventor in 342 US patents or patent applications in a range of technologies, from actual computer and portable devices to user interfaces (including touch-based), speakers, keyboards, power adapters, staircases, clasps, sleeves, lanyards, and packages.

Jobs's contribution to most of his patents was "the look and feel of the product." Most of these are design patents (specific product designs; for example, Jobs listed as primary inventor in patents for both original and lamp-style iMacs, as well as the PowerBook G4 Titanium) as opposed to utility patents (inventions). He has forty-three issued US patents on inventions. The patent on the Mac OS X Dock user interface with "magnification" feature was issued the day before he died. However, Jobs had little involvement in the engineering and technical side of the original Apple computers.

Even while terminally ill in the hospital, Jobs sketched new devices so that users could hold the iPad in a hospital bed. He also despised the oxygen monitor on his finger and suggested ways to revise the design for simplicity.

The Macintosh Computer

The Macintosh was introduced in January 1984. The computer had no "Mac" name on the front, but rather just the Apple logo. It had a friendly appearance and was meant to be user-friendly. The disk drive was below the display, and the Macintosh was taller, narrower, more symmetrical, and suggestive of a face. The Macintosh was identified as a computer ordinary people could understand.

The NeXT Computer

When Jobs was forced out of Apple in 1985, he started a company that built workstation computers. The NeXT Computer was introduced in 1989. Sir Tim Berners-Lee created the world's first web browser on the NeXT Computer. The NeXT Computer was the basis for today's Macintosh OS X and iPhone operating system (iOS).

iMac

Introduced in 1998, the Apple iMac's innovative design was directly the result of Jobs's return to Apple. Apple boasted, "The back of our computer looks better than the front of anyone else's." Described as "cartoon-like," the first iMac, clad in Bondi blue plastic, was unlike any personal computer.

In 1999, Apple introduced the graphite-gray Apple iMac and since has switched to all white. Design ideas, such as the handle and a breathing light effect when the computer went to sleep, were intended to create a connection with the user. The iMac sold for $1,299 at that time. There were some technical revolutions for iMac too. The USB ports were the only device inputs on the iMac, and iMac's success helped popularize the interface among third-party peripheral makers, which is evidenced by the fact that many early USB peripherals were made of translucent plastic to match the iMac design.

iPod

The first generation iPod was released on October 23, 2001. The major appeal of the iPod was its small size—achieved by using a 1.8-inch hard drive, compared to the 2.5-inch drives common to players at the time. The capacity of the first generation iPod ranged from five to ten gigabytes. The iPod sold for US$399, and more than one hundred thousand iPods were sold before the end of 2001.

With the introduction of the iPod, Apple became a major player in the music industry, iPod's success preparing the way for the iTunes music store and the iPhone. After the first generation iPod, Apple released the hard-drive-based iPod classic, the touchscreen iPod Touch, a video-capable iPod Nano, and the screenless iPod Shuffle in the following years.

iPhone

Apple began its work on the first iPhone in 2005, and the first iPhone was released on June 29, 2007. The iPhone created such a sensation that, according to one survey, six out of ten Americans were aware of its release. *Time* magazine declared this small device—with multimedia capabilities and functions such as a quad-band touch-screen smartphone—Invention of the Year.

Jobs died at his California home around 3 p.m. on October 5, 2011, due to complications from a relapse of islet-cell neuroendocrine pancreatic cancer. He had lost consciousness the day before, and died with his wife, children, and sister at his side.

Both Apple and Microsoft flew their flags at half-staff throughout their respective headquarters and campuses. And Bob Iger ordered all Disney properties, including Walt Disney World and Disneyland, to fly their flags at half-staff from October 6th to the 12th.

Jobs may have left the earth, but his legacy lives on. When *Time* named his computer as the 1982 "Machine of the Year," it published a long profile of Jobs as "The most famous maestro of the micro."

Steve Wozniak

I could fill a few pages with information on Wozniak, but most of it has already been covered in the section about Steve Jobs. "Woz," as he is affectionately known, was the technical brains behind the Apple's design and when he worked on something, it typically performed spectacularly. He is credited with single-handedly inventing both the Apple I and Apple II computers during the 1970s.

Though he withdrew from the University of California, Berkeley, a year after enrolling in 1971, Woz *did* eventually earn his bachelor's degree in 1983, seven years after the founding of Apple.

Writing

Writing is a field where you'd think degrees would matter, along with fields such as engineering, science, and the medical professions; however, many of our greatest writers achieved success and widespread fame *without* a university-approved education.

Let's take a look at a few.

William Faulkner

William Faulkner was born on September 25, 1897. He was a writer and Nobel Prize laureate from Oxford, Mississippi. Faulkner wrote poetry and screenplays but is primarily known for his novels and short stories set in a fictional county, although it was supposedly based on the place he spent most of his life.

Faulkner is one of the most celebrated writers in American literature generally and in Southern literature specifically. He originally published his work in the early 1900s, but he didn't achieve fame until he won the 1949 Nobel Prize in Literature, for which he became the only Mississippi-born Nobel winner.

Two of his works, *A Fable* (1954) and his last novel, *The Reivers*

(1962), won the Pulitzer Prize for Fiction. In 1998, the Modern Library ranked his 1929 novel, *The Sound and the Fury*, sixth on its list of the one hundred best English-language novels of the twentieth century; also on the list were *As I Lay Dying* (1930) and *Light in August* (1932). *Absalom, Absalom!* (1936) is often included on similar lists.

In school, Faulkner excelled in first grade, skipped second, and continued doing well through the third and fourth grades. However, somewhere in the fourth and fifth grades of his schooling, Faulkner became a much more quiet and withdrawn child. He began to play hooky occasionally and became somewhat indifferent to his schoolwork, even though he began to study the history of Mississippi on his own time in the seventh grade. His declining performance in school continued over the years, and Faulkner wound up repeating the eleventh, and then final grade, and then never graduating from high school.

In his early twenties, Faulkner would give poems and short stories he had written to his friend Stone, in hopes of having them published, but Stone would send them to publishers only to be rejected.

In 1918, Faulkner himself made the change to his surname from the original "Falkner." According to one story, however, a careless typesetter simply introduced the error. When the misprint appeared on the title page of his first book, Faulkner was asked whether he wanted a change. He supposedly replied, "Either way suits me."

During his adolescence, Faulkner began writing poetry almost exclusively. He did not write his first novel until 1925. His literary influences are deep and wide. He once stated that he modeled his early writing on the Romantic era of late eighteenth- and early nineteenth-century England. He attended the University of Mississippi ("Ole Miss") in Oxford, enrolling in 1919, and attended three semesters before dropping out in November 1920. William was able to attend classes at the university due to the rules on nepotism— his father had a job there as a business manager. He skipped classes often and received a D grade in English. However, some of his poems were published in campus journals.

Writing

From the early 1920s to the outbreak of World War II, when he left for California, Faulkner published thirteen novels and many short stories. Such a body of work formed the basis of his reputation and led to his being awarded the Nobel Prize at age fifty-two. Faulkner's prodigious output, mainly driven by an obscure writer's need for income, includes his most celebrated novels—*The Sound and the Fury* (1929), *As I Lay Dying* (1930), *Light in August* (1932), and *Absalom, Absalom!* (1936). Faulkner was also a prolific writer of short stories.

He was known for his experimental style, with meticulous attention to diction and cadence. In contrast to the minimalist, understated style of his contemporary Ernest Hemingway, Faulkner made frequent use of "stream of consciousness" in his writing and often wrote highly emotional, subtle, cerebral, complex, and sometimes Gothic or grotesque stories about a wide variety of characters, including former slaves, descendants of slaves, poor white folk, agrarian or working-class Southerners, and Southern aristocrats.

In an interview with the *Paris Review* in 1956, Faulkner remarked: "Let the writer take up surgery or bricklaying if he is interested in technique. There is no mechanical way to get the writing done, no shortcut. The young writer would be a fool to follow a theory. Teach yourself by your own mistakes; people learn only by error. The good artist believes that nobody is good enough to give him advice. He has supreme vanity. No matter how much he admires the old writer, he wants to beat him."

I have never cared for Faulkner's writing, but I'm not here to argue writing styles or preferences. He was undoubtedly a talented man. No one wins a Nobel Prize without talent. The question is, how did he get that way? Was it environment?

No matter how you look at it, the "education" he received was *not* from the university.

Edgar Allan Poe

An early proponent of the short story and father of modern detective novels, Edgar Allan Poe was one of first authors to earn a living from writing alone—or at least he tried to. Poe was born in Boston in 1809. He also spent time in Philadelphia, Richmond, and Baltimore before he died in Baltimore in 1849 at age forty.

Poe dropped out of University of Virginia due to a lack of funding and was expelled from the US Military Academy.

Influence
For such an "unsuccessful" businessman, Poe has had widespread influence. His works were devoured in Europe, especially France, and he is now considered to be the "Father of the Modern Detective Story" (and inventor of the detective genre); in fact, the Mystery Writers of America even name an annual award—The Edgar—after

him. The award is presented to the author who has produced "outstanding work in the mystery field."

If you have read any of his popular works, there can be no doubt of the man's talent. The short story—*A Telltale Heart*, is a classic, as is *The Raven*, certainly one of his most accomplished poetical works.

But Edgar Allan Poe is not a man to model your life after. He was an alcoholic, among other things, and struggled financially his entire life. But there can be no denying his talent, and that came from inside the man. It was not nurtured at a university or by a professor of literature; it was molded by Poe's own life experiences.

Jane Austen

Jane Austen was an English (UK) novelist known primarily for six of her novels (two more were published posthumously):

- *Pride and Prejudice*
- *Sense and Sensibility*
- *Persuasion*
- *Emma*
- *Northanger Abbey*
- *Mansfield Park*

Austen didn't write a lot of novels, but those she did write were good, and she remains one of the most respected novelists the world over.

She did not achieve fame during her lifetime, but there is hardly a bookstore, online or off, that doesn't stock her works today—almost two hundred years after her death.

All five of her major novels were published for the first time between 1811 and 1818. She wrote two additional novels, *Northanger Abbey* and *Persuasion*, both published posthumously in 1818, and began another one, which was eventually titled *Sanditon*, but died before completing it.

In the last one hundred years, Austen's works have endured worldwide criticism and, as a result, she has gained worldwide fame, albeit posthumously. Her books have inspired filmmakers for the past seventy years and have attracted such actors as Laurence Olivier and Emma Thompson.

Education

In 1783, Jane and her sister, Cassandra, were sent to Oxford to be educated by Mrs. Ann Cawley; however, both of girls caught typhus, and Jane nearly died and was sent home to be educated. By December 1786, both sisters returned home because the Austens could not afford to send their daughters to school. Jane finished her education by reading books.

Even though Jane did not have a formal education, she was by no means uneducated. She possessed a keen sense of people's personalities, society's manners, and she had a magnificent flair for the written word. Novels don't survive two hundred years without being singular. The test of time is best, and Jane has survived that test. I feel certain that two hundred years from now people will still be reading *Pride and Prejudice*, as well as her other works.

Mark Twain

Samuel Langhorne Clemens (November 30, 1835–April 21, 1910), better known by his pen name, Mark Twain, was an American author and humorist. Among his writings are *The Adventures of Tom Sawyer* (1876) and its sequel, *The Adventures of Huckleberry Finn* (1885), the latter often called "The Great American Novel."

In 1865, his humorous short story, "The Celebrated Jumping Frog of Calaveras County," was published. It was based on a story he heard at the Angels Hotel in Angels Camp, California, where he spent some time as a miner. The story brought international attention and was even translated into classic Greek. His wit and satire, in prose and in speech, earned him praise from critics and peers, and he was a friend to presidents, artists, industrialists, and European royalty.

Twain was lauded as the greatest American humorist of his age. William Faulkner even called Twain the "father of American literature."

Twain moved to San Francisco in 1864 as a journalist and met writers such as Bret Harte and Artemus Ward. A year later he traveled to the Sandwich Islands (present-day Hawaii) as a reporter for the *Sacramento Union*. His letters to the *Union* were popular and became the basis for his first lectures.

In 1867, a local newspaper funded a trip to the Mediterranean. During his tour of Europe and the Middle East, he wrote a popular collection of travel letters, which were later compiled as "The Innocents Abroad" (1869). It was on this trip that he met his future brother-in-law, Charles Langdon. Both were passengers aboard the *Quaker City* on their way to the Holy Land. Langdon showed a picture of his sister Olivia to Twain, who claimed to have fallen in love at first sight.

Upon returning to the United States, Twain was offered honorary membership in Yale University's secret society, Scroll and Key, in 1868. Its devotion to "fellowship, moral and literary self-improvement, and charity" suited him well.

Twain's novel *A Connecticut Yankee in King Arthur's Court* (1889) features a time traveler from the contemporary US using his knowledge of science to introduce modern technology to Arthurian England. This type of storyline would later become a common feature of the science fiction subgenre alternate history.

In 1909, Thomas Edison visited Twain at his home in Redding, Connecticut, and filmed him. Part of the footage was used in *The Prince and the Pauper* (1909), a two-reel short film. It is said to have been the only known existing film footage of Twain.

Twain was in great demand as a featured speaker, performing humorous talks similar to what would later become stand-up comedy. He was paid to give talks to many men's clubs, including the Authors' Club, Beefsteak Club, Vagabonds, White Friars, and Monday Evening Club of Hartford.

In the late 1890s, he spoke to the Savage Club in London and was elected an honorary member. When told that only three men had been so honored, including the Prince of Wales, he replied, "Well, it must make the Prince feel mighty fine."

Oxford University awarded Twain an honorary doctorate in letters (D. Litt.) in 1907. Officials in Connecticut and New York estimated the value of Twain's estate at $471,000 ($12,000,000 today).

Summary

Twain began his career writing light, humorous verse, but he evolved into a chronicler of the vanities, hypocrisies, and murderous acts of mankind. At midcareer, with *Huckleberry Finn*, he combined rich humor, sturdy narrative, and social criticism.

Twain was a master at rendering colloquial speech and helped to create and popularize a distinctive American literature built on American themes and language. Many of Twain's works have been suppressed at times for various reasons.

The Adventures of Huckleberry Finn has been repeatedly restricted in American high schools for its frequent use of the word "nigger," though it was common usage in the pre-Civil War period in which the novel was set.

Regardless of Twain's use of now-banned words, it takes nothing away from his talent as a writer or from his insight. He had a unique ability to get to the bottom of a person's personality and summarize it in a few short words. Twain also brought a *depth* to his characters few writers are able mimic. It's why his books are still read and enjoyed after all this time.

Ernest Hemingway

Hemingway made Shakespeare's saying "Brevity is the Soul of Wit" a lifelong ambition. His writing style is not only copied and taught by many, there is now an app named after Hemingway that analyzes writing and provides advice for unnecessary words.

Ernest Hemingway was born on July 21, 1899, in Oak Park, Illinois. He died on July 2, 1961.

Notable Awards

Nobel Prize in Literature (1954)

Hemingway was an American novelist, short-story writer, and journalist. His economical, understated style had a strong influence on twentieth-century fiction, while his life of adventure and his public image influenced later generations.

Hemingway produced most of his work between the mid-1920s and the mid-1950s, and won the Pulitzer Prize for Fiction in 1953 and the Nobel Prize in Literature in 1954. He published seven novels, six short story collections, and two nonfiction works. Additional works, including three novels, four short-story collections, and three nonfiction works, were published posthumously. Many of his works are considered classics of American literature.

Education and Early Life

Hemingway attended River Forest High School, where he served as part-time editor of the school newspaper. After high school, he went to work for the Kansas City Star as a cub reporter. Although he stayed there for only six months, he continued to refer to the *Star*'s style guide as a basis for his writing: "Use short sentences. Use short first paragraphs. Use vigorous English. Be positive, not negative." This is how the Kansas City Star style sheet began.

Hemingway would make these rules a lifelong quest as he perfected his talent, and to this day his work is a model for concise writing. A 1926 *New York Times* critique of his first work said it best: "No amount of analysis can convey the quality of *The Sun Also Rises*. It is a truly gripping story, told in a lean, hard, athletic narrative prose that puts more literary English to shame."

Another critic said of Hemingway's style that it "changed the nature of American writing."

In 1954, when Hemingway was awarded the Nobel Prize for Literature, it was for "his mastery of the art of narrative, most recently demonstrated in *The Old Man and the Sea*, and for the influence that he has exerted on contemporary style." (That from the Novel Board)

Ernest Hemingway never finished college, but who is to say if it would have helped him? If he hadn't gone to the *Kansas City Star*, perhaps he would have never been introduced to concise writing, and his own *style* would not have developed.

Millions of today's writers are doing their best to emulate Hemingway. As mentioned, even an app is named after him. I hope those millions remember they're focusing on a man who never received a degree.

Here are a few of Hemingway's selected works:

- *The Sun Also Rises (1926)*
- *Fifty Grand (1927)*
- *Men Without Women (1927)*
- *A Farewell to Arms (1929)*
- *Death in the Afternoon (1932)*
- *Green Hills of Africa (1935)*
- *The Snows of Kilimanjaro (*First published in 1936 in Esquire magazine).
- *To Have and Have Not (1937)*
- *For Whom the Bell Tolls (1940)*
- *The Old Man and the Sea (1951)*

A number of Hemingway's books were made into movies:

- *To Have and Have Not*, starring Humphrey Bogart and Lauren Bacall
- *For Whom the Bell Tolls* starred Gary Cooper and Ingrid Bergman
- *The Snows of Kilimanjaro*, with Gregory Peck and Susan Hayward
- *The Sun Also Rises* starred Tyrone Power and Ava Gardner
- *The Old Man and the Sea*, with Spencer Tracy

Most writers would cut off their right arm to have even one of their books made into a movie. Hemingway had a slew of them, and it continues. As recently as 2010, *The Garden of Eden* was made into a movie, and some, like *the Old Man and the Sea*, have even been remade.

The Arts (Painting and Sculpting)

Leonardo da Vinci

Leonardo di ser Piero da Vinci is widely known as Leonardo da Vinci; however, da Vinci indicates *where* he was from, not his family surname. It means "Leonardo, from the town of Vinci" (or *of* the town of Vinci).

Anyway, he was born in 1452 near Florence and died in 1519. He is regarded by many to have been the most intelligent and talented man to have ever lived, and is the prime example of the *Renaissance man.*

He was the consummate inventor and one of the greatest artists of all time. The *Mona Lisa* and *The Last Supper* are but two examples of his talent. Few people go through life without seeing a representation of one or both. But he wasn't just an inventor or painter, he also had interests in sculpting, mathematics, music, architecture, science, writing, anatomy, engineering, botany, astronomy, cartography, and many others areas. He has been called the father of paleontology and architecture, and is sometimes credited with the invention of the parachute, helicopter, and tank.

Many historians and scholars say Leonardo had an "unquenchable curiosity" and a "feverishly inventive imagination." According to

Helen Gardner, in the *History of Western Art—Revised*, "The scope and depth of his interests were without precedent," and "his mind and personality seem superhuman."

A few of his notable works, include the *Mona Lisa, The Last Supper, The Vitruvian Man,* and *Lady with an Ermine.*

Leonardo was educated in the studio of Florentine painter Vercocchio, and never received a *formal* education. Yet he made substantial discoveries in anatomy, civil engineering, optics, and hydrodynamics. He did not publish his findings, but word got around, and he was highly sought after by the Medici, the Sforzas, and the Borgias (three of the most powerful families of the time).

They used Leonardo for his talents in sculpting, painting, invention, and Cesare Borgia (who was the son of Pope Alexander VI—I know, popes aren't supposed to have sons) used him for his cartography skills as well as in other military engineering matters.

In 1516, King Francis I brought Leonardo to France, where he would live out the last few years of his life. After he died, Francis supposedly said (according to the UK Telegraph), "There had never been another man born in the world who knew as much as Leonardo." (And, remember, this was during a time when men knew a hell of a lot.)

The interest and excitement in Leonardo's genius continues to this day. In 1994, Bill Gates, bought Leonardo's *Codex Leicester,* a manuscript that dates back to the sixteenth century. He paid $30.8 million for the journal at auction, making it the most expensive book ever sold.

Michelangelo Buonarroti

Michelangelo was born in 1475, near present-day Florence. His birth name was Michelangelo di Lodovico Buonarroti Simoni. He died in 1564 at the age of eighty-eight.

He is best known for his sculpting and for his painting of the ceiling of the Sistine Chapel in the Vatican, but he is also respected for his architecture and poetry. At the age of seventy-four, he succeeded Antonio da Sangallo as the architect of St. Peter's Basilica, in Rome.

Notable works include:

- *David*
- *Pietà*
- *The Last Judgment*
- *Sistine Chapel* ceiling

He is often compared to Leonardo, and in the view of many critics, rightly claims the title of the premier Renaissance man. His interests were not as broad as Leonardo's; however, there is no denying his talent regarding painting or sculpting. One look at *David, Pietà, The Last Judgment,* or the *Sistine Chapel* ceiling is all you need to know that he was a master.

Despite the presence of *La Gioconda* (the *Mona Lisa*), many critics considered Michelangelo the greatest living artist of his time and one of the greatest artists of all time. Regardless of your stance, there is no questioning his influence on Western art.

When Michelangelo was six, his mother died, and he was sent to live with a stonecutter and his family. It was during this time that

Michelangelo developed his love for sculpting and his talent with hammer and chisel.

Michelangelo was sent to Florence for schooling, but he had no love for it and ended up finding work in the arts, painting and sculpting. He eventually landed a role with Lorenzo de Medici, and settled in for his studies. The statue of *David* (1504) is one of the greatest works of the Renaissance.

Around that time (1500), Michelangelo completed his sculpture of the *Pietà*. It would soon be thought of as one of the world's greatest masterpieces. The great Vasari said, "It is certainly a miracle that a formless block of stone could ever have been reduced to a perfection that nature is scarcely able to create in the flesh." Even Michelangelo's detractors had to admit it was stupendous. (Quote source in The Civilization of the Italian Renaissance: A Sourcebook By Kenneth R. Bartlett)

These accomplishments were made by a man who never received formal schooling. Yes, I realize that formal schooling was not as commonplace as it is today, but it was certainly not unusual. Michelangelo simply had interests in other things, and he fervently pursued them. In the process, through dedication and perseverance, he became one of the most respected artists and sculptors of all time.

Summary

We have analyzed a substantial list of people from a variety of industries and fields, and yet we haven't even touched the surface. There are hundreds, if not thousands, of examples in the United States alone.

If you examine the list of the world's wealthiest people, one thing is immediately apparent—five of the top ten do not have degrees; even numbers one and two (Gates and Gaona) do not. So how is it that the world's richest man and the world's second richest man do *not* have degrees? And how is it that 32 percent of the world's billionaires do not? That's thirty-two percent, almost one in three! (According to a Fortune magazine article in 2016, there are 740 people without degrees who are billionaires)

Of the top ten most valuable companies in the world, numbers one, two, and five (Apple, Exxon, and Microsoft) were founded by people on our list (Jobs/Wozniak, Rockefeller, and Gates/Allen).

Also look at Larry Ellison (number seven on the list). He founded and ran Oracle, the second largest software company in the world (Microsoft, run by Bill Gates, is the largest). How is it that the two largest software companies were founded and run by non-degreed people? Wouldn't you think that would require an *education*? Or take a look at Amancio Ortega, who went from delivery-boy to running the world's largest fashion empire.

The one thing all of these people have in common is that none of them possessed degrees (a few, like Wozniak, did get degrees later). Some dropped out of college, and some never went at all, but none was awarded a degree, unless you count honorary degrees, which were bestowed on several of them. (Perhaps it's a statement that degrees *can* be bought.)

The one thing these people *did* have in common was a strong desire to succeed and a drive, with perseverance accompanying that drive. When they saw something and believed it was right, they *went* for it. They didn't give up. Didn't quit. Refused to accept failure.

That doesn't mean no one failed. They did. What it means is that they got up afterward and tried again. *That's the way to greet failure— with a toothy grin and a grim determination.*

I said at the beginning of this book that I wasn't against formal education, and I'm not. I think formal education offers some people many advantages, including camaraderie, a structured learning environment, and (for the most part) competent instructors. Some people, however, can experience most of that on their own, and perhaps they're not ready for the school environment.

Should they be penalized? Should they be restricted from jobs because they don't have a piece of paper stating they received a degree? How much better is the college athlete whose professors let them skate by so they might contribute to the sport's program?

A quick scan of the wealthiest people reveals that of the non-degreed members in the top ten, all got there by founding their own companies, which invites the question—How many would have been hired by other companies for a substantial position?

Probably none. And that raises a bigger question—Why not?

The likely answer is a simple one. Most job descriptions call for degrees, and some call for advanced degrees. The problem is that the people writing those job descriptions have no idea why.

I've seen dozens of project management job descriptions that require a master's or PhD, and for no reason. In seven of those cases, we filled the jobs with bachelor-degreed people, and in one case, with a non-degreed person. I recently checked, and five years after the fact, they were all performing wonderfully.

The degrees weren't needed at all; the companies simply *thought* they were needed. (We probably could have filled most of the jobs with non-degreed people, but the other companies wouldn't even consider the possibility.)

A survey conducted by Bloomberg in 2010 shows that the school of hard knocks was the *number-one* source of education (tied with the University of California) for the CEOs of S&P 500 companies. Harvard was number-three (along with the universities of Texas, Missouri, and Wisconsin). The school of hard knocks features CEOs who never graduated from college.

Of the top 400 richest Americans in 2011, 27 graduated from high school but did not attend college. Another 36 were college dropouts.

That's 63 out of 400—almost 15 percent—a pretty significant number.

We've considered only a small sampling here. For a more complete list of people who have "made it" without degrees, check out this site: (http://www.collegedropoutshalloffame.com. Courtesy of John Kremer of Open Horizons) or look at the list below (partially taken from John's site).

Regarding the names, I included only those I felt people would recognize or who were important enough to include, even if not recognized.

S. Daniel Abraham, billionaire founder of Slim-Fast. He joined the army at the age of eighteen and fought in Europe during World War II. He never attended college.

Gautam Adani, commodities billionaire from India. Dropped out of college.

Sheldon Adelson, billionaire casino owner. Dropped out of City College of New York to become a court reporter. He made his first fortune doing trade shows.

Ben Affleck, actor, screenwriter. Left the University of Vermont after one semester, then dropped out of Occidental College to pursue a career in acting. He cowrote *Good Will Hunting* with Matt Damon and won an Academy Award. He also won Best Picture for a film he directed, *Argo*, and two Golden Globes. I've heard people say "He can't act," or comments like that. I disagree. Look at films like *Good Will Hunting*, *The Town*, *Argo*, etc. He not only acted well but directed or wrote part of the screenplay. It takes a lot more than raw talent to do that, so kudos to Ben for hanging in there.

Christina Aguilera, singer, songwriter. Never finished high school. You can say, "She has talent, so it was easy to make it," or whatever else you want, but she also had the courage to persevere. Not many people do, degree or not.

Dennis Albaugh, billionaire founder of pesticide company Albaugh, Inc. Earned a two-year agriculture business degree from Des Moines Community College. Did not continue on to a four-year degree.

Harold Alfond, billionaire founder of the Dexter Shoe Company, which he sold for a stake in Berkshire Hathaway. He never went to college.

Joy Alukkas, billionaire jeweler. Never attended college. Immediately after high school, he moved to the Gulf to open a jewelry store.

Dhirubhai Ambani, billionaire Indian businessman. High school dropout.

Wally "Famous" Amos, multimillionaire cookie entrepreneur, author, talent agent. Dropped out of high school at the age of seventeen to join the US Air Force. Wally didn't learn this in the Air Force, according to him. Who's to say though, he might have been inspired or had discipline instilled in him by the Air Force.

As far as the idea, though, he probably thought this up one night in bed, or one morning in the shower, like many of us do. The difference is he acted on his idea. He *did* something about it. And he stayed with it until he was successful.

Tom Anderson, cofounder of MySpace. A high school dropout. Some say this was a precursor to Facebook. Regardless, it was wildly successful at the time, and like almost all social media platforms (Facebook, Twitter, Whatsapp, Tumblr, Wordpress, etc.), it was founded by a non-degreed person.

Jennifer Aniston, actress. She never attended college. Some people have said she has made it on her looks alone. I say, who cares. Who doesn't want to see Jennifer Aniston? Aside from how gorgeous she is, she is reportedly worth about $170 million (CNW). To get that much money, she had to do something right, or hire someone to do it right. Either way, it's a darn nice accomplishment.

Micky Arison, billionaire chairman of Carnival Cruise Line, owner of the Miami Heat NBA team. He dropped out of the University of Miami.

Julian Assange, Wikileaks founder, software programmer. He attended several schools, but did not complete a degree.

John Jacob Astor, multimillionaire businessman and America's first multimillionaire. He dropped out of high school. I think it says something (though I don't know what) that America's first multimillionaire had no degree.

David Baazov, multimillionaire CEO of PokerStars and Cadillac Jack. Bored at school, he dropped out at the age of sixteen. (Among an age of billionaires, "multimillionaire" has lost some of its impact, but still, it's a hell of an accomplishment. I'm willing to bet "multimillionaire" still outshines most of us.)

Jimmy Santiago Baca, poet, activist, and filmmaker. At a young age, he ran away from the orphanage and lived on the streets, spending some time in juvenile detention centers. Before he was imprisoned for seven years for a narcotics conviction (a charge he's denied), he was functionally illiterate. During his time in prison, he taught himself to read and write, eventually earning a GED. Now Baca has written ten books of poetry, a memoir, a book of essays, a book of short stories, a play, and a screenplay for the 1993 film Bound by Honor.

Bill Bartman, billionaire businessman, author. High school dropout. (Later in life, he earned a degree.) In October 2013, "Bouncing Back" the autobiography of Bill Bartmann's life was published (Brown Books), detailing Mr. Bartmann's unlikely life story from homelessness and abject poverty to Nobel Peace prize nominee. It became an Amazon number one best seller.

Eike Batista, billionaire mining executive. Studied metallurgy at the University of Aachen, Germany. Dropped out. Rose to become one of the richest men in the world (in excess of $20 billion), lost it all, and since then has started rising again.

Heinz-Georg Baus, billionaire founder of the German home-improvement retail chain Bauhaus AG. Here's a man you have to give credit. He was a carpenter who went on to open a home-improvement store. Opening one store and making it a success is amazing enough, but turning it into a hugely profitable retail chain takes it to another level.

Andrew Beal, billionaire banker and real estate investor. He left Michigan State when he was twenty to renovate and flip apartment buildings. He later founded Beal Bank, a Texas bank with $3.6 billion in deposits.

Glenn Beck, radio and TV political commentator, best-selling book author. Enrolled at Yale University for one class but quickly dropped out.

Anne Beiler, multimillionaire cofounder of Auntie Anne's Pretzels restaurants. High school dropout.

Tony Bennett, aka Anthony Benedetto, singer, artist. Attended New York City's High School of Industrial Art but dropped out at the age of sixteen to support his family. Bennett has been performing for sixty-plus years. That alone is a special kind of dedication, but Tony's had the willpower to do this night after night for all of these years, and since he was a teenager! And he didn't learn that in college.

Irving Berlin, Oscar Award–winning songwriter, composer. Wrote such long-lasting hits as *God Bless America*, *White Christmas*, and *There's No Business Like Show Business*.

Carl Bernstein, Watergate reporter, *Washington Post*. Never finished college. Started as a copy boy at the *Washington Star* at the age of sixteen. Here's a guy who took perseverance to another level. He got onto a story and wouldn't let go. As a result, a president was impeached and politics was changed forever.

Halle Berry, Oscar Award–winning actress. After high school, she moved to Chicago to pursue a career in modeling. Did not attend college.

Patrizio Bertelli, billionaire cofounder of Prada fashion house. Dropped of engineering school to produce leather belts and handbags. And he has done it with perfection. What woman do you know who doesn't want something made by Prada?

Manoj Bhargava, billionaire founder of 5-Hour Energy. He dropped out of Princeton University and returned to India to spend twelve years as a monk. He later developed the formula that made him rich. I don't know what's in the drink, but do I need to? All I really need to know is that Bhargava had the marketing savvy to sell it.

Timothy Blixseth, billionaire founder of Yellowstone Club. Skipped college, failed as a professional songwriter. Made his first fortune as a timberland investor. At the age of fifteen he bought three donkeys for seventy-five dollars and resold them a week later as pack mules. Blixseth has had his share of ups and downs. Recently, he spent fourteen months in prison for failing to abide by a civil order regarding disclosing the disposal of assets.

Humphrey Bogart, Oscar Award–winning actor. He flunked out of prep school at Andover.

Alain Bouchard, billionaire cofounder of the Alimentation Couche-Tard convenience store chain (including the Circle K stores in the United States). Never attended college. Began working at the age of nineteen in one of his brother's stores.

Ray Bradbury, award-winning science-fiction author. Never went to college because his parents couldn't afford to send him, so he sold newspapers on Los Angeles street corners by day and educated himself at libraries by night. "I never went to college. I went to the library."

He graduated from the library at the age of twenty-eight. This is a guy who wouldn't quit. He wouldn't say no, and you have to admire him for that. He could have committed murder and I would still admire his persistence in educating himself and then using that knowledge to become successful.

Joseph Brodsky, Nobel Prize–winning Russian poet and essayist, Poet Laureate of the United States from 1991 to 1992. Left school at the age of fifteen and tried to enter the School of Submariners but was not accepted.

Edgar Bronfman Jr., billionaire heir to the Seagram liquor fortune. Skipped college to pursue a career as a songwriter and movie producer but soon began running the Seagram corporation.

Charles Bronson, actor. He was ten when his father died, and he went to work in the coal mines to help support the family.

Gisele Caroline Bündchen, Brazilian multimillionaire supermodel. She is a high school dropout. She left home at the age of fourteen to begin her modeling career. She moved to New York City at the age of sixteen to continue that career.

Ronald Burkle, billionaire supermarket owner and investor, the Yucaipa Companies. Dropped out of California State Polytechnic University and returned home to work in a Stater Brothers grocery store. Had started stocking shelves; joined union as a box boy at age thirteen.

James Francis Byrnes, US representative, US senator, Supreme Court justice, US secretary of state, South Carolina governor. At the age of fourteen, he left St. Patrick's Catholic School to apprentice in a law office. Never attended college or law school. It's tough enough to be elected to the Senate or to be appointed a Supreme Court justice or secretary of state, but to do so without having a degree is an accomplishment few people can boast of. And Byrnes did it after leaving school at the age of fourteen!

James Cagney, actor, song-and-dance man. Worked from the age of fourteen as an office boy, janitor, package wrapper, and finally vaudeville dancer. He was well-liked by almost everyone who worked with him, and at his funeral Ronal Reagan, who was then the President of the United States, delivered the eulogy.

Michael Caine, Oscar Award–winning actor. Dropped out of high school.

James Cameron, Oscar Award–winning director, producer, and screenwriter. Dropped out of California State University, Fullerton, at the age of twenty.

To be a successful director in Hollywood requires a lot of dedication (and brains). Cameron seems to have it all. He is the director of films such as, *Terminator, Aliens, Terminator II, Titanic,* and *Avatar*. *Titanic* and *Avatar* are the two highest grossing films of all time, and two of only three films to have exceeded $2 billion. Cameron's net worth is pegged at about $650 million.

Andrew Carnegie, industrialist and philanthropist. Elementary school dropout. Started work at the age of thirteen as a bobbin boy in a textile mill. One of the first mega-billionaires in the United States. Carnegie was the epitome of success. Enough said.

Scott Carpenter, astronaut. He twice flunked out of the University of Colorado.

Julia Carson, US Congress representative. Did not graduate from college. She was the first woman and first African American to represent Indianapolis.

Tom Carvel, inventor of the soft-serve ice cream machine, founder of Carvel ice cream stores. Did not attend college. Before he began selling ice cream, he was an auto mechanic, Dixieland band drummer, and test driver for Studebaker.

Pete Cashmore, founder of Mashable.com. Founded the blog website when he was nineteen. Did not complete college. Retired from active blogging three years later.

John Catsimatidis, billionaire oilman and real estate magnate, founder of Red Apple supermarkets. Studied engineering at New York University but dropped out to help a friend save his family's supermarket business. Owned ten stores by age twenty-four, with $25 million per year in income.

Bruce Catton, historian, author, editor of *American Heritage*. World War I interrupted his studies at Oberlin College. He tried twice after the war to finish but kept getting pulled away by real jobs at a succession of newspapers.

Herb Chambers, billionaire car dealer. He dropped out of high school during his senior year to join the navy. At age twenty-two he started as a copier repairman at $75 per week. Before long, he built that business into that million-dollar enterprise that became world's largest dealer of Canon and Minolta copiers, with a workforce of more than 1,400. Later, he bought into car dealerships and now owns fifty-five of them. Not bad for a young man from the South of Boston. It's quite an accomplishment for anyone but especially for someone who dropped out of high school.

Jackie Chan, actor and philanthropist. A grade school dropout, he attended the China Drama Academy, became an accomplished student of martial arts and acrobatics, and began working in films at the age of eight. He spent the years after high school doing construction jobs before finally becoming a successful actor.

John Chancellor, TV journalist and anchorman. He dropped out of high school.

Subhash Chandra, billionaire founder of Zee TV satellite television channel. He dropped out of college to help his family. He became a rice trader and later founded Essel Propack.

Coco Chanel (Gabrielle Bonheur Chanel), fashion designer. She left the orphanage at the age of eighteen to pursue a career as a cabaret singer.

Do Won Chang, billionaire cofounder of the Forever 21 retail chain. He never attended college.

Jin Sook Chang, billionaire cofounder of Forever 21 retail chain. She never attended college.

Mack Chase, billionaire founder of Mack Energy. He began working on oil rigs when he was fourteen years old and then served as a mechanic during the Korean War only to return home to work on oil wells with his father and brother. He never attended college.

Binod Chaudhary, Nepal's first billionaire, hotel owner, banker, and more. He skipped college to join his family trade at the age of eighteen.

Maurice Chevalier, Oscar Award–winning actor, singer. Dropped out of high school.

Winston Churchill, British prime minister, historian, artist. Rebellious by nature, he generally did poorly in school. Flunked sixth grade. After he left Harrow, he applied to the Royal Military Academy at Sandhurst, but it took him three times before he passed the entrance exam. He graduated eighth out of a class of 150 a year and a half later. *He never attended college.* Churchill rose to the occasion when England was in dire straits. Many countries have been led by non-degreed people, but I doubt any needed someone more than Britain needed Churchill during WWII. He served as an inspiration when inspiration was needed most.

Grover Cleveland, US president (twenty-second and twenty-fourth). Dropped out of school to help his family. Studied law while clerking at a law firm.

Paulo Coelho, songwriter, best-selling novelist. Was institutionalized from age seventeen to age twenty. He later enrolled in law school but dropped out after one year, became a hippie, traveled the world, and later worked as a songwriter before writing his first novel.

It's not easy to write a novel. I know. I've done it. But Coelho did more than write a novel; he wrote *The Alchemist*, which has sold about 100 million copies internationally and holds the Guinness World Record for most translated book by a living author.

I don't know how many authors can claim to have achieved sales of more than 100 million copies , but I know it's not many, so kudos to Paulo. (By the way, it was a damn good book.) According to CNW, he is worth approximately $500 million. Though not the most books ever sold, it has sold one hell of a lot.

Bram Cohen, software programmer, developer of BitTorrent. He attended the State University of New York at Buffalo for one year and then left.

Jack Kent Cooke, billionaire media mogul, owner of the Washington Redskins football team. He dropped out of high school. He also was the owner of the Los Angeles Lakers (NBA), the Los Angeles Kings (NHL), and the Los Angeles Wolves (United Soccer Association).

James Fenimore Cooper, novelist. He was kicked out of college for a prank.

Al Copeland, multimillionaire founder of Popeye's Fast Food (Louisiana Chicken). Left high school at the age of sixteen to work in a supermarket and later at a doughnut shop.

Cindy Crawford, actress, model, entrepreneur. Graduated high school as valedictorian, then studied chemical engineering at Northwestern University for half a year before dropping out to model. Would she have looked any better with a degree? *Could she?*

Tom Cruise, actor, producer. Never attended college.

Roy Cullen, oilman billionaire. Though he dropped out of school before the sixth grade, Cullen obviously learned *something*. He went on to become an amazingly successful businessman, and later in life established a foundation that helped support the University of Houston. He also donated land to Texas Southern University for their campus. When he died, his net worth was about $300 million. All in all, that's not bad for someone who never finished sixth grade.

Charles Culpeper, multimillionaire owner and CEO of Coca-Cola. Dropped out of high school. He was at first a salesman, then bought the New Jersey and New York bottling companies for Coca Cola.

Brunello Cucinelli, billionaire fashion designer. Dropped out of engineering school. "In three years I completed one exam."

Chris Dawson, billionaire cofounder of The Range discount stores (along with his wife Sarah). Having never learned to read until the age of twenty-seven, he had dropped out of school at the age of fifteen and started selling cookware in open-air markets. He had built that one store into a chain of about 150, and has been wildly successful.

Darwin Deason, billionaire entrepreneur, founder of ACS. Left his hometown the day after graduating from high school for Tulsa,

Oklahoma, where he got into data processing. Later took over MTech, which he sold in 1988.

John Paul DeJoria, billionaire cofounder of John Paul Mitchell Systems hair care products and founder of Patrón Spirits tequila, Gustin Energy, DeJoria Diamonds, ROK Mobile, and other companies. He joined the US Navy right out of high school. After the navy, he spent time doing many odd jobs, sometimes even living out of a car, before finding work selling hair care products.

Leonardo Del Vecchio, billionaire founder of Luxottica. He began as an apprentice to a tool and dye maker of molds for auto parts and eyeglass frames. Skipping college, he started Luxottica at the age of twenty-three. Leonardo started out simple but saw an opportunity needing to be addressed. Luxottica is now the world's largest manufacturer of prescription eyewear and sunglasses. You can't beat that for ambition or perseverance.

Chances are that if you are wearing a nice pair of sunglasses, they were either made or licensed by Luxottica. Here are some of their brands: Ray-Ban, Oakley, Vogue Eyewear, Persol, Oliver Peoples and Alain Mikli

Richard DeVos, billionaire cofounder of Amway (now Alticor), owner of the Orlando Magic basketball team. Founded Amway with his best friend Jay Van Andel.

Leonardo DiCaprio, actor. At the age of fourteen, he signed with an agent and began doing commercial work as well as acting. He completed high school with a tutor but put off college. As he has noted, "Life is my college now." Besides being a tremendously accomplished actor, he is an outspoken environmentalist and a proponent of solar engineering. He has a net worth of more than $240 million. His recent win of Best Actor at the 2016 Academy Awards will go a long way in increasing his net worth.

Charles Dickens, best-selling novelist. Although he had little formal education, his early poverty drove him to succeed. Dickens was one of the most beloved novelists of all time, yet he never finished elementary school. Instead, he went to work in a factory when his father was thrown into debtors' prison. He is highly regarded by readers and other authors, and is considered the most accomplished author of the Victorian era.

Barry Diller, billionaire, Hollywood mogul, Internet maven, chairman of IAC/InterActive Corp (owner of Ask.com, Match.com, OkCupid, Ticketmaster, CitySearch, Evite, LendingTree.com, and more). He attended Beverly Hills High School, then UCLA, but dropped out after four months to work in the mail room of William Morris. He has also worked at ABC, Paramount, and Fox, overseeing the development of hits like *Cheers* and *The Simpsons*.

Walt Disney, producer, director, screenwriter, animator. Winner of twenty-six Oscars and seven Emmy awards. While attending McKinley High School, he also took night classes at the Chicago Art Institute, but he dropped out of high school at the age of sixteen to join the army. Rejected because he was under age, he joined the Red Cross and was sent to war in Europe. Upon his return from war, he began his artistic career. Walt Disney was the founder of Disney Studios and the developer of Disneyland and DisneyWorld, two of the world's most popular vacation destinations.

Charles Dolan, billionaire founder of HBO, which he traded to Time Inc. for Cablevison cable provider. He also owns Madison Square Garden, the New York Knicks, and the New York Rangers. He dropped out of college.

Jack Dorsey, billionaire founding CEO of Twitter, cofounder and CEO of Square. He dropped out of New York University twice and bounced between jobs before landing at Odeo, the forerunner of Twitter. Dorsey made more than a few bucks on Twitter, and rightfully so. He recognized an opportunity and took advantage of it. Don't you think it's interesting that social media and technology in general have been dominated by non-degreed people?

George Eastman, multimillionaire inventor and founder of Kodak. High school dropout.

Clint Eastwood, Oscar Award–winning actor, director, and producer. Attended at least half a dozen schools and excelled at none of them. Enrolled at Los Angeles City College, but never graduated. Among other jobs, he bagged groceries, delivered papers, fought forest fires, and dug swimming pools. He also was a steelworker and logger. Few can doubt the talent of Eastwood. All you have to do is watch some of the early spaghetti Westerns, but it took a lot to go from actor to successful director and to mayor of a California city (Carmel).

John Edson, billionaire leisure-craft manufacturer. Dropped out of the University of Washington. Started building boats in his garage.

Daniel Ek, cofounder of Spotify, software engineer. After high school, he enrolled at the Royal Institute of Technology in Sweden to study engineering. After eight weeks, he dropped out. Via programming, he became a millionaire by the age of twenty-three.

Larry Ellison, billionaire cofounder of Oracle software company. He dropped out of the University of Chicago after one year. Later, he also dropped out of the University of Illinois at Urbana-Champaign, but then he discovered computer programming. He started out life in a broken home, and was soon given up for adoption. He became fascinated with relational databases after he moved to California as a young man, and not long after that cofounded Oracle. Now, Ellison is the third richest person in the US, and (according to *Forbes)* is estimated to be worth about $50 billion.

Eminem, rapper. He has a limited formal education, but, he says, "By the time I was 18 I had probably read the dictionary front to back like 10 times."

Tom Epperson, novelist and screenwriter. After taking a few classes at Henderson State University in Arkansas, he dropped out and headed for New York City to become a novelist. Four years later, he headed to Los Angeles to write screenplays.

Shawn Fanning, developer of Napster. Dropped out of Northeastern University when nineteen to move to Silicon Valley to further develop Napster. He made the cover of both *Time* and *Fortune* months before he dropped out of school! Fanning's idea of an easy way to share music may or may not have contributed to the idea for iTunes, but regardless, it was an idea whose time had come.

Arash Ferdowsi, cofounder of DropBox.com. Dropped out of MIT to start up DropBox.com. His net worth is estimated at $400 million.

Enzo Ferrari, founder of the Scuderia Ferrari Grand Prix motor racing team and later the Ferrari car manufacturer. Grew up with little formal education. A Ferrari is all about perfection. One look at one, and you'll know.

Tilman Fertitta, billionaire owner of Landry's restaurants and Golden Nugget casinos. Dropped out of both Texas Tech University and the University of Houston. I think the number of restaurants he owns is now more than 500. In 2015 *Forbes* called him the "World's Richest Restaurateur". Fertitta is also chairman of the Board of Regents of the University of Houston System, a bit of irony considering he has no degree.

Debbi Fields, founder of Mrs. Fields Cookies. She founded the company when she was a twenty-one-year-old mother with no business experience. She did not graduate from college. Fields' experience goes to show that common sense still plays a part in being successful—a big part.

Millard Fillmore, US president. With only six months of formal schooling, he studied law while a legal clerk for a judge and law firm. Of the forty-three people who served as president of the United States, twelve never went to college. Some may argue that it doesn't take much to run the country, and I won't argue that point at this time, but I believe it takes even more to get elected to the position of running the country. For that, I give Fillmore and all the others like him a hell of a lot of credit.

Paul Fireman, billionaire owner of Reebok. He dropped out of Boston University to take over his family's sporting-goods business. Anytime that a person drops out of school to "take over" a family business, it's usually due to a catastrophe of some kind. Regardless of why Fireman did what he did, Reebok was the beneficiary. Fireman has built it to be a profitable and successful company.

Harvey S. Firestone, industrialist and founder of Firestone Tires. After graduating from Columbia High School in Ohio, he worked for a buggy company before starting his own company making rubber tires for carriages. Ten years later he started Firestone Tire and Rubber Company to make tires for automobiles.

Bobby Fischer, Grandmaster chess player and high school dropout. At age thirteen Fischer won a "brilliancy" that became known as "The Game of the Century."

Starting at age fourteen, Fischer played in eight US Championships, winning each by at least a one-point margin. At fifteen, Fischer became both the youngest Grandmaster up to that time and the youngest candidate for the World Championship. At age twenty, Fischer won the 1963–64 US Championship with 11/11, the only perfect score in the history of the tournament. Fischer's *My 60 Memorable Games* (1969) remains a revered work in chess literature.

Competing in a field many consider to be dominated by intellectuals and by the use of intellectual strategy, Fischer became the best. He is considered by many to be the greatest chess player of all time.

F. Scott Fitzgerald, novelist. He dropped out of Princeton University. He also wrote one of the most "required-reading" books in school, *The Great Gatsby*.

Charles Foley, inventor of the Twister party game and ninety-six other inventions. Dropped out of school after the eighth grade and served in the Michigan Air National Guard before getting a job at a design studio.

Henry Ford II, CEO, Ford Motor Company. Dropped out of Yale University.

Donald Friese, billionaire CEO of C.R. Laurence. He has never attended college.

Robert Frost, poet. He dropped out of Dartmouth College.

R. Buckminster Fuller, visionary, philosopher, poet, architect, futurist, and inventor of the geodesic dome. After being expelled from Harvard twice (one of those times involving some chorus girls), he never finished college.

J. B. Fuqua, industrialist, philanthropist. Never attended college but learned about business by checking out books from the Duke University library through the mail. Later donated $36 million to support a business school at Duke.

Lady Gaga, aka Stefani Joanne Angelina Germanotta, rock singer and songwriter. Dropped out of NYU at the age of nineteen to pursue her music career full-time.

Amancio Ortega Gaona, billionaire fashion entrepreneur, second richest man in the world. Born in poverty, he could not afford to go to college. He dropped out of high school and at fourteen, got a job at a local clothing store. He went on to found and build the Zara retail empire, which now consists of more than 6,000 stores and more than 90,000 employees. He is estimated to be worth about $77 billion dollars, eclipsed only by Gill Gates in wealth.

David Geffen, billionaire founder of Asylum Records and Geffen Records and cofounder of DreamWorks. A dyslexic, he dropped out of the University of Texas at Austin after his freshman year. He also flunked out of Brooklyn College.

Peter Gelb, general manager of the Metropolitan Opera. He dropped out of Yale University after less than a month.

Alan Gerry, billionaire cable TV executive, philanthropist. He dropped out of high school during World War II to join the Marines. In 1956, he launched his cable business with $1,500.

George Gershwin, songwriter, composer. High school dropout.

J. Paul Getty, billionaire oilman, once the richest man in the world. Failed to graduate from the University of Southern California, Berkley, or from Oxford University. Why is it that several of the world's richest men have been non-degreed? No matter the reason— what they've done has been one hell of an accomplishment.

Amadeo Peter Giannini, multimillionaire founder of Bank of America. High school dropout. Giannini was one of the first bankers to offer banking services to middle-class Americans, rather than only the upper class. He began offering his services to the Italian immigrants, then, as business boomed, he expanded. Initially, his business was named the Bank of Italy. Later, he changed it to the Bank of America.

He also pioneered the holding company structure and established one of the first modern trans-national institutions

William Gibson, science-fiction novelist, first to use the word *cyberspace*. He never attended college.

Daniel Gilbert, psychology professor at Harvard University. Dropped out of high school but later earned an equivalency diploma.

John Glenn, astronaut, US senator. Did not finish at Muskingum College in Ohio. "In April 1959, despite the fact that Glenn failed to earn the required college degree, he was assigned to the National Aeronautics and Space Administration (NASA) as one of the original group of Mercury astronauts."

Sam Goi, billionaire owner of Tee Yih Jia Food Manufacturing, the Popiah King. Dropped out of school to work at his father's grocery store.

Hyman Golden, multimillionaire cofounder of Snapple. A high school dropout and one-time window washer. Goes to show that anyone can get thirsty, but only a few know how to turn that thirst into a business—especially a thriving, successful business.

Barry Goldwater, US senator and presidential candidate. So he dropped out of the University of Arizona after one year, took over the family business, became a senator, and ran for president. Not bad. Whether you like his politics or not, he did what few can do.

Berry Gordy is the founder of Motown Records. He is responsible for recruiting raw talent off the streets of Detroit and forming them into musical groups people love to listen to. Some of his early successes were The Supremes, The Temptations, Smokey Robinson and the Miracles, Marvin Gaye, and many others. Today, Gordy's net worth is said to be about $350 million.

Johann Graf, billionaire gambling mogul. He started out as an apprentice in a butcher shop before he started importing pinball machines. He never attended college.

Laurence Graff, billionaire jeweler. At the age of fifteen, he was apprenticed to a London jeweler. He never attended college.

David Green, billionaire founder of Hobby Lobby. Did not attend college. Took a $600 loan and turned other people's hobbies into a business that made him a billionaire. Pretty crafty (pun intended).

Philip Green, billionaire retail mogul, Topshop. Dropped out of high school to apprentice with a shoe importer.

Thomas Haffa, billionaire German media mogul. He dropped out of high school.

Bruce Halle, billionaire founder of Discount Tire Company. During the Great Depression, he delivered newspapers, cut grass, and dug graves. He later served in the Marines. He did not attend college.

Harold Hamm, billionaire oil wildcatter, Continental Resources, Hiland Holdings. He left home at the age of seventeen and got married but finished high school a year later. He became a gas jockey before becoming a wildcatter. He later took college classes in geology, chemistry, and mineralogy but never graduated.

Tom Hanks, Oscar Award–winning actor. He graduated from Chabot Community College in Hayward, California and then attend CalState University but dropped out after about a year to work as an intern at the Great Lakes Theater Festival.

Sean Hannity, radio and TV talk-show host. He spent three years in college, but when the money ran out, he dropped out and went into the construction business.

Louise Hay, one of the best-selling authors in history and founder of Hay House. Of other famous women authors, Levine Breaking News has noted, "They did not change the spiritual landscape of America and several of its Western allies. They were not pregnant at 15 and they did not lack high-school diplomas." Louise Hay encountered all of these obstacles.

William Randolph Hearst, newspaper publisher and movie producer, was thrown out of Harvard for his poor grades (apparently due to heavy partying). Hearst built one of the world's biggest media empires, among other things, and he did it all without a degree. The Hearst Castle on the drive from Los Angeles to San Francisco is still a must stop.

Amanda Hocking, multimillionaire self-publisher, novelist, blogger. She had only a few months of college. Amanda was one of the first of the self-published success stories. She went from writing a few short stories to selling millions of books, and it seems as if she accomplished it overnight. Forget the writing, although that took skill—it's her business savvy that impresses me. She's done a great job and earned herself a nice publishing contract in the bargain.

Elizabeth Holmes, billionaire founder and CEO of Theranos. As a sophomore, she left Stanford University's School of Engineering to build Theranos around her patents and a vision for healthcare. There are people who question Elizabeth's motivation and say the technology doesn't work. If she knew beforehand it didn't work, that's one thing, but if she thought it worked and was able to secure funding in such a competitive market, more power to her.

Mark Hughes, multimillionaire founder of Herbalife. He dropped out of high school after the ninth grade. He launched Herbalife at the age of twenty-four.

Haroldson Lafayette Hunt, billionaire oilman. Only had a fifth-grade education. Worked as a farmhand until he invested fifty dollars in an Arkansas oil field.

Jim Jannard, billionaire founder of Oakley and inventor of the Red One digital camera. He dropped out of USC School of Pharmacy to found Oakley and he sold it years later for $2 billion to another non-degreed member on the list (Luxottica owner).

Peter Jennings, news anchor, *ABC World News Tonight*. Failed the tenth grade. Left high school at sixteen to work as a bank teller. He later attributed his failure in high school to boredom and laziness. But it doesn't matter what he attributed his failure in high school to—failure is failure. What's impressive is that he was able to pick himself up and move ahead until he made it. That shows spirit. It's one thing to fail—everyone does it—it's quite another to come back from failure and succeed. Few do that.

Billy Joel, singer and songwriter—and high school dropout.

Jón Jóhannesson, founder of Baugur Group fashion retailing group, finished Commercial College in Iceland (the equivalent of something between high school and junior college in the United States) and then launched a discount grocery with his father.

Andrew Johnson, US president, vice president. Never attended college. Remember, of the forty-three people who served as president of the United States, twelve never went to college. Johnson had the added distinction of having to assume duties for Abraham Lincoln after he was assassinated.

Travis Kalanick, billionaire founder and CEO of the Uber ride-sharing service. He dropped out of UCLA a few months before graduation to join the founding team of Scour. After a lawsuit, the company filed for bankruptcy and then moved on to start Uber, which now has sales approaching $2 billion.

Dean Kamen, multimillionaire inventor of the Segway. He dropped out of Worcester Polytechnic Institute.

Ingvar Kamprad, billionaire founder of IKEA, and one of the richest people in the world. A dyslexic, he never attended college. When he was seventeen, his father gave him a reward for succeeding in his studies. He used this money to establish what became IKEA. As a child, he peddled matches, Christmas decorations, fish, and other sundries via his bicycle.

With annual sales of approximately $12 billion and 375 stores worldwide, IKEA is truly an international company.

David Karp, billionaire founder of Tumblr. At the age of eleven he taught himself how to write code. He dropped out of Bronx Science at the age of fifteen to be homeschooled and went to work for his own software consulting company, Davidville. He never attended college. At the age of seventeen, he moved to Japan and worked remotely for an American Internet company. He founded Tumblr at the age of twenty.

As I was researching for this book, it seemed as if every technology and social media platform worth its salt was founded by non-degreed people. Tumblr is no different. Though not as famous as Facebook or Twitter, Tumblr still gets more than 500 million visitors per month and hosts about 240 million blogs, and Karp is worth in excess of $200 million. Not bad for a kid who never attended college.

Li Ka-Shing, billionaire, one of the wealthiest investors in Asia, plastics manufacturer, real estate investor. He had to leave school at the age of twelve to work in a plastics factory in order to support his family after his father's death. He never attended college.

Kirk Kerkorian, billionaire investor and casino operator, owner of MGM movie studio, Mirage Resorts, and Mandalay Bay Resorts. He dropped out of the eighth grade to pursue amateur boxing. He later trained fighter pilots during World War II. After the war, he founded Trans World Airlines. Kerkorian died in 2015. He had done a lot with his life, including amateur boxing, training fighter pilots, operating casinos, and running airlines. What he didn't do was go to college, and yet his net worth at the time of his death was about $4 billion.

Thomas Kincade, the painter of light, inspirational speaker, house designer. He attended the University of California at Berkeley and the Art Center College of Design for brief periods but dropped out to become a set painter in Hollywood.

Robert Kirkman, comic-book writer, producer. After graduating from high school, he went right into creating comic books by founding his own publishing company, Funk-O-Tron. He later worked for Image Comics, where he developed *The Walking Dead* series, which ultimately led to the creation of the TV series of the same name.

Michael Kors, billionaire fashion designer. He dropped out of fashion school.

Ray Kroc, multimillionaire founder of McDonald's. High school dropout. When I go to McDonald's, no matter where it is—in Kansas City or Buffalo—I *know* it will taste the same. The reason for that lies mainly with founder Ray Kroc, who also owned the San Diego Padres for almost a dozen years.

Bernard Kroger, founder of Kroger supermarkets. Went to work at the age of thirteen to help support his family. Never attended college. With more than 375,000 employees and 2,700 locations, Kroger is the largest grocery store in the US, by revenue ($109.83 billion for fiscal year 2015), the second-largest general retailer (behind Walmart), and twenty-third largest company in the United States. Kroger is also the fifth largest retailer in the world.

When you shop there, you're concerned with price, employee efficiency, and how fresh the food is. It doesn't matter if the founder has a degree or not, does it?

Stanley Kubrick, movie director and producer, screenwriter, photographer. His poor high school grades made it impossible to attend college.

Frederick "Freddy" Laker, billionaire airline entrepreneur. He dropped out of high school.

Edwin Land, inventor of the Polaroid camera, founder and CEO of Polaroid. In 1937, he dropped out of Harvard to work on his light polarization inventions. His technological breakthroughs included infrared night-vision products, instant-color film, and the Polaroid camera.

Cathy Lanier, chief of police in Washington, DC. She was a fourteen-year-old pregnant high school dropout and a mother at fifteen.

On August 16, 2016, it was announced that Lanier will retire from the Metropolitan Police Department of the District of Columbia in September 2016 to become Senior Vice President of Security for the National Football League. Her last day was September 15, 2016.

Queen Latifah, aka Dana Elaine Owens. Singer, songwriter, rapper, actress, television producer, record producer, talk-show hostess. She never attended college. She has won the following awards: Golden Globe, Grammy Award, Screen Actors Guild (and been nominated for many more).

Christos Lazari, billionaire real estate investor. At the age of sixteen, he dropped out of high school and moved from Cyprus to England where he began working as a dishwasher.

Mike Lazaridis, billionaire founder of Research in Motion, which manufactured and designed the Blackberry, the phone that originally began the craze for smartphones.

Harper Lee, Pulitzer Prize–winning author, *To Kill a Mockingbird*. Dropped out of college during her senior year. Moved to New York to become a writer.

Stan Lee, comics creator, Marvel Comics (*Spiderman, The Hulk, X-Men, The Fantastic Four*). Started working when he was still in high school. Never attended college. Lee is one of the most respected people in the comics business, and not just because of his artistic skills. He has an ability to determine what people will like. Movie franchises are still being created on the comics and characters developed by him.

James Leprino, billionaire, Leprino Foods. Joined the family business at the age of eighteen and turned it into the world's largest mozzarella producer.

Doris Lessing, novelist. At the age of fourteen, she chose to end her formal schooling. She then worked as a nanny, telephone operator, office worker, stenographer, and journalist. Her first novel was published when she was thirty-one. She won the Nobel Prize for Literature in 2007.

Aaron Levie, multimillionaire software developer, cofounder of Box.net. Dropped out of the University of Southern California in 2005 to create Box.net.

Phil Liblin, CEO of Evernote. He dropped out of Boston University to found and sell two startups. If you haven't used Evernote, you should. And if you have, you know what a genius Liblin is.

Rush Limbaugh, multimillionaire media mogul, the most popular radio talk-show host ever, best-selling author. Dropped out of college after being required to take ballroom dancing. Love him or hate him, give him credit. He has created one hell of a business.

Carl Lindner, billionaire investor, founder of United Dairy Farmers, former owner of Chiquita Brands. Dropped out of high school at the age of fourteen to deliver milk for the family store during the Depression.

Marcus Loew, multimillionaire founder of Loews movie theaters, cofounder of MGM movie studio. Dropped out of elementary school.

Jack London, best-selling novelist. He dropped out of high school to work. Later he was admitted to the University of California but left after one semester to join the Klondike Gold Rush. He was one of the first fiction writers to obtain worldwide celebrity and a large fortune from his fiction alone. He also established one of the best 'personalities' of any character on his dog in *The Call of the Wild*.

Sophia Loren, aka Sofia Scicolone, Oscar Award–winning actress, author, model. She dropped out of elementary school. Although known for 'other traits' it was her acting ability that eventually won her international fame. Her performance in *Two Women* was classic, among others.

Tom Love, billionaire founder of Love's Travel Stops. After dropping out of the University of Oklahoma, he and his wife opened a gas station in Watonga, Oklahoma. They later opened a convenience store. They now operate more than three hundred travel stops in thirty-nine states.

Luiz Inácio Lula da Silva, Brazilian president. With a fifth-grade education only, he shined shoes on the streets of Sao Paulo as a kid but later became a steelworker union leader.

Susan Lyne, journalist, editor in chief, Hollywood executive, multimedia mogul.

Mary Lyon, education pioneer, teacher, founder of Mount Holyoke College (America's first women's college). Dropped out of high school. Started teaching at the age of seventeen. Mount Holyoke is a world-renowned institution, but what would it have been without the influence of Mary Lyon? It's something to think about.

John Mackey, founder of Whole Foods and developer of Conscious Capitalism. He dropped out of the University of Texas six times. He never took a business course.

Harry Macklowe, billionaire real estate developer. He dropped out of college to become a real estate broker.

John Major, British prime minister. High school dropout.

Henning Mankell, author of forty books. At the age of sixteen, he made a decision to go to the university of life, leaving school and traveling to Paris to become a writer

David Marcus, founder of mobile payment company Zong, CEO of PayPal. He dropped out of the University of Geneva to work at a bank to help support his family.

Dean Martin (Dino Crocetti), singer, actor, comedian. He never finished high school. Dean did almost everything before he became a singer. He was a bootlegger, a blackjack dealer, and even a boxer. Later he became one of the only people to ever hold simultaneous records for the number-one spot in movies (with Jerry Lewis), in nightclubs, on the music charts, and on TV (the *Dean Martin Show*). Dean died in 1995. At the time of his death he was reportedly worth about $30 million. Not bad for those days. And certainly not bad for a kid from the 'wrong side of town.'

Andrew Mason, cofounder of Groupon. Was offered $1 million by his partner to quit college and begin working on the daily deal website.

Konosuke Matsushita, multimillionaire founder of Panasonic. At the age of ten, he was apprenticed to a hibachi store in Osaka, Japan.

Robert Maxwell, billionaire publisher. He dropped out of high school.

Craig McCaw, billionaire founder of McCaw Cellular. He dropped out of college, and built McCaw into a profitable business.

Billy Joe (Red) McCombs, billionaire founder of Clear Channel media empire, car dealerships, real estate investor. He dropped out of law school to sell cars in 1950. He owned his first automobile dealership by the age of twenty-five.

Herman Melville, a mid19th century novelist. He is best known for *Moby Dick,* and a novella he wrote, *Billy Budd.* He was a high school dropout. Don't you find it odd, that a guy who had no degree wrote two books (*Moby Dick* and *Billy Budd)* that became required reading in thousands of schools?

Rosalia Mera, cofounder of the fast-fashion retail giant Zara. She left school to work as a seamstress before founding Zara with her then-husband, Amancio Ortega, who is the second richest person in the world.

Cesar Millan, aka "The Dog Whisperer," and reality TV show star. Has not attended college. This is a man who took his love and passion for dogs and turned it into a thriving business. In the process, he has helped thousands of animals. What more could you want?

Art Modell, NFL football team owner, Cleveland Browns and Baltimore Ravens. His father died when he was fourteen, and he became a high school dropout at the age of fifteen. Modell used his success in sales and advertising to propel himself to a position where he could purchase the franchise for the Cleveland Browns in 1961. He functioned as the owner until 1996.

Nirav Modi, billionaire jeweler. Dropped out of Wharton to work with his uncle in India.

Dustin Moskovitz, billionaire cofounder of Facebook social network. Dropped out of Harvard. Anyone who drops out of Harvard better have something damn good to go to. Mokovitz obviously thought he did, and he thought right. According to Celebrity Net Worth, he is worth approximately $10 billion. Not bad no matter which school you dropped out of.

Wolfgang Amadeus Mozart, classical music composer and performer. In his early years, his father taught him music, languages, and other academic subjects. From the age of six, he performed alongside his older sister in cities all over Europe. He never attended high school or college.

Matt Mullenweg, founder of WordPress. He dropped out of the University of Houston to take a job at CNET Networks. He later cofounded WordPress, Automattic, Akismet, Polldaddy, Gravatar, Vault Press, and more online services. About 74 million sites use Wordpress to power their blogs. It's easy to use and is universally recognized—and all the result of Matt Mullenweg's ingenuity.

James Murdoch, billionaire CEO of Fox Entertainment. He left Harvard University to start Rawkus Entertainment, a rap music label.

David Murdock, billionaire real estate investor, chairman of Dole Foods. He is currently funding a $1.5 billion health research campus in North Carolina. He dropped out of high school in the ninth grade and began working at a gas station until he was drafted into the army in 1943. He never attended college.

Walter Nash, prime minister of New Zealand. He dropped out of high school.

David Neeleman, founder of JetBlue airlines. Dropped out of the University of Utah after three years.

Jack Nelson, Pulitzer Prize–winning journalist. Never attended college. After high school, he went to work for the *Biloxi Daily*

Herald. Later, he opened the Atlanta bureau of the *Los Angeles Times* and later became the *Times*'s bureau chief in Washington, D.C.

Donald Newhouse, billionaire publisher, Advanced Publications. He dropped out of Syracuse University.

Jean Nidetch, founder of Weight Watchers. After graduating from high school, she went to work for the IRS. After an embarrassing encounter in a supermarket where her friends thought she was pregnant, she started up the Weight Watchers program as a support group. She never attended college. Would Weight Watchers be around if not for Jean's embarrassing encounter? Probably so, but most likely in a different form and fashion. Let's just thank God for Jean, as her company has helped millions.

Xavier Niel, computer programmer, Internet billionaire, chairman of Free Mobile and Kima Ventures venture capital firm. He has no college degree.

David Ogilvy, advertising copywriter and executive. Was thrown out of Oxford University at the age of twenty in 1931 during the Great Depression. Began working as a lowly cook in a hotel restaurant. Eventually became a world-class chef. Left that job to sell upmarket kitchen stoves, which led to a job in advertising.

Fred Olsen, billionaire oil driller, oil rig builder, renewable energy, and owner of Timex, Fred Olsen Energy, Fred Olsen Cruise Lines, Fred Olsen Renewables, and Fred Olsen Ocean; also a world-champion sailor. Instead of attending college, he worked on his family's ships for two years. As he noted of that experience, "No diploma could come close to that education."

David Oreck, multimillionaire founder of the Oreck Corporation, which builds those wonderful vacuum cleaners. He not only figured out how to build a great vacuum cleaner, he figured out how to sell them.

George Orwell (aka Eric Blair), author of *Animal Farm* and *1984*. Instead of attending university after graduating from Eton, he joined the Imperial Police and worked in Burma. When he returned, he worked in restaurant kitchens, slept in homeless shelters, and eventually documented the condition of miners. All the while, he was writing reviews, essays, novels, and a regular newspaper column. His *Animal Farm* has sold more than 10 million copies. Orwell gets to join our celebrated club of authors—Hemingway, Mark Twain, Edgar Allan Poe, Jane Austen, William Faulkner, etc.

Fred Otash, celebrity detective. Left home to join the Marines before joining the Los Angeles Police Department. Later became a detective for Hollywood celebrities.

Sean Parker, billionaire cocreator of Napster, founding president of Facebook.com. He barely finished high school (he was not interested in school). Never made it to college. According to the 2014 book, *You Only Have to Be Right Once,* Parker said, "I kind of refer to it as Napster University. It was a crash course in intellectual property law, corporate finance, entrepreneurship, and law."

Jeno Paulucci, multimillionaire founder of Chun King and Jeno's. Left school at the age of sixteen to sell fruits and vegetables. Twenty years later he borrowed $2,500 to begin canning his own version of chow mein. He sold Chun King 11 years later for $63 million. Several years later, he founded Jeno's where he created pizza rolls. He sold that company 17 years later for $140 million.

Markus Persson, billionaire game developer of Minecraft. He did not finish high school. The next time you are ready to chide your children for playing games, think of Persson, who is now a billionaire. And he probably had fun building the company.

Stefano Pessino, billionaire, CEO of Walgreens Boots Alliance drugstores and pharmaceutical wholesaler. He attended the Politecnico di Milano but dropped out when he was disgusted with the lax grading standards. I'm sure that now he doesn't have to worry about those standards.

Pablo Picasso, modern artist, painter, sculptor, cofounder of Cubism, co-inventor of collage. At the age of sixteen, he attended the Royal Academy of San Fernando (Spain's foremost art school), but he disliked the formal instruction and soon quit attending classes altogether.

Mary Pickford, Oscar Award–winning actress, cofounder of United Artists. Six months of formal education. Homeschooled.

François Pinault, third-richest man in France, billionaire owner of Gucci, Samsonite, Puma, and Christie's auctions. He quit high school to work at his father's lumber mill.

Chet Pipkin, billionaire founder of Belkin. He dropped out of UCLA after less than a year to invent personal computer accessories. And there aren't many avid computer users who haven't plugged in a Belkin product.

Eugene Polley, inventor of the wireless remote control. Attended the City Colleges of Chicago and the Armour Institute of Technology (now the Illinois Institute of Technology) but did not have enough money to graduate from college. Joined Zenith as a parts clerk at the age of twenty and rose from the stockroom to the engineering department based on his mechanical aptitude. Eventually earned eighteen US patents for his inventions.

Ron Popeil, multimillionaire founder of Ronco, inventor, infomercial pitchman, and producer. Dropped out of college. He did, though, receive the Ig Nobel Award for Consumer Engineering. Inventor of the Solid Flavor Injector, Mr. Microphone, Showtime Rotisserie, and more.

Terry Pratchett, best-selling fantasy author. He sold his first short story at the age of fifteen (and immediately bought his first typewriter). After he dropped out of school, he worked as a journalist while writing fantasy novels on the side. Pratchett has sold more than 85 million books. Even at ten cents a book, that's eight and a half million dollars, and I'm sure he earned more than ten cents a book.

Azim Premji, chairman of Wipro. Dropped out of Stanford University to rush home to India to take care of his family after his father died. Built Wipro into a multibillion-dollar company. Many years later he completed his Stanford degree via correspondence course. "If my father had not died, I probably would have stayed in the U.S. and completed my master's degree."

Usher Raymond IV, quadruple platinum singer. He won the Star Search male teen vocalist competition when he was eighteen. He was signed to a music label immediately thereafter. Usher not only has produced a long string on musical successes, he also is part owner of the Cleveland Cavaliers (who just won a championship), and he had the smarts to agree to represent Justin Bieber.

Louis Renault, founder of the Renault Auto Company. Failed the exams for the École Centrale. But with the financial backing of his brothers, he founded his first auto factory.

Lynda Resnick, billionaire cofounder of POM Wonderful; also co-owner of Fiji Water, Teleflora, and Halos mandarin oranges. A child actress, Lynda dropped out of Los Angeles City College to start an advertising agency at the nineteen. She and her husband are one of the country's largest producers of pomegranates, pistachios, almonds, and mandarin oranges.

Marc Rich, billionaire commodities investor, built Philbro into the world's largest commodities firm, founded Marc Rich & Co. Dropped out of NYU to take a job in the mail room of Philipp Brothers on Wall Street.

Leandro Rizzuto, billionaire founder of Conair. Dropped out of college to found Conair with a $100 investment and the invention of a hot-air hair roller invention.

Nevaldo Rocha, billionaire founder of the Guararapes Confeccoes fashion empire. Never attended high school.

Kjell Inge Rokke, billionaire Norwegian businessman. No secondary or college education. Started out as a fisherman at the age of eighteen.

George Romney, automotive executive, Michigan governor, presidential candidate. Spent only a year at the University of Utah.

Kevin Rose, founder of Digg.com, TechTV host. Dropped out of the University of Las Vegas during his sophomore year to code software. He wrote his first software program in the second grade and was building his own machines by the beginning of high school. He started Digg with $1,200, launching the site from his bedroom.

Renzo Rosso, billionaire cofounder of Diesel jeans. Joined Italian fashion manufacturer Moltex at the age of twenty; owned 40 percent of the business by the age of twenty-two. Renamed the company Diesel in 1978.

Karl Rove, presidential advisor. Left the University of Utah after two years to work for the college republicans.

Frederick Henry Royce, multimillionaire cofounder of Rolls-Royce, automotive designer. Elementary school dropout.

Michael Rubin, billionaire founder of e-commerce company GSI Commerce and Kynetic (including ShopRunner, Rue La La, and Fanatics). He dropped out of Villanova University after six months to continue to operate several ski shops he had opened as a teenager.

Phillip Ruffin, billionaire casino operator. He dropped out of Wichita State to flip burgers. With the money he saved, he invested in convenience stores, oil, and real estate. Eventually he got into casinos. The best day of his life? August 10, 2007. The day he put $1.24 billion into his checking account. (According to an answer to questions asked by *Forbes* in a 2007 article)

Haim Saban, billionaire producer of the *Mighty Morphin Power Rangers* TV show. He also owns stakes in Univision and Paul Frank Industries. He was kicked out of agricultural boarding school and soon joined the Israeli Army. He never attended college.

William Safire, columnist for *The New York Times*. Dropped out of Syracuse University to take a job as a researcher for a column.

Edmond Safra, billionaire banker, philanthropist. High school dropout.

J. D. Salinger, novelist, *Catcher in the Rye* (with over 60 million copies sold so far). Briefly attended Ursinus College and New York University before publishing short stories in *Collier's* and *Esquire*. Salinger has earned the honor of securing a spot on the top one hundred best-selling books of all time. *Catcher in the Rye* sits at about number twelve on the list, with over 60 million copies sold. There are plenty of proud recipients of MA degrees in Arts and Literature who would kill to have their books sell that many copies.

Silvio Santos, billionaire TV host, the first ever Brazilian celebrity billionaire. He started out as a street vendor in Rio de Janeiro. Apparently did not attend college.

Jose Saramago, Nobel Prize–winning novelist. He graduated from trade school and then studied literature mostly on his own. Since he won the Nobel Prize, I will assume that his lack of a formal education did not hurt him too much.

Cherilyn Sarkisian, aka Cher, singer, Oscar Award–winning actress. Dropped out of high school in the eleventh grade and started taking acting lessons. At sixteen, she moved out of her house. Soon she met Sonny Bono, and the two formed Sonny and Cher, created many hits, and starred in *The Sonny and Cher Comedy Hour*.

David Sarnoff, radio and TV producer. High school dropout.

William Saroyan, Oscar Award–winning screenwriter, Pulitzer Prize–winning playwright. High school dropout. There aren't many who can claim to be an Oscar Award–winning screenwriter, let alone a Pulitzer Prize–winning playwright, but Saroyan can, and he doesn't even have a degree.

Ari Sason dropped out of the University of Buffalo and worked out of his home to help his brother Joshua Sason found the investment company Magna Group.

Vidal Sassoon, multimillionaire founder of Vidal Sassoon hairstyling salons and hair-care products. High school dropout.

Nick Schorsch, billionaire founder of American Realty Capital Properties. He dropped out of college and never returned.

Richard Schulze, billionaire founder of Best Buy. After high school and a stint in the Air National Guard, he sold electronics for his father's distribution company and later opened a car-stereo shop. He never attended college. Best Buy is the largest consumer electronics company in the US. It has more than 1,900 stores and locations, including large-format and Best Buy Mobile stores. The company also offers technical support under the Geek Squad brand. They made a name for themselves by being one of the first companies to offer technically-competent salespeople to help customers.

Maurice Sendak, best-selling children's book author and illustrator. He never attended college. He had a number of odd jobs before landing a job as a window dresser at the FAO Schwartz toy store in New York City. His first book illustrations were published when he was nineteen years old.

William Shakespeare, playwright, poet. He had only a few years of formal schooling.

George Bernard Shaw, playwright, author. High school dropout.

Yasumitsu Shigeta, billionaire founder of mobile phone distributor Hikari Tsushin and a medical insurance provider. He dropped out of college.

Walter Shorenstein, billionaire real estate investor, Shorenstein Properties. He dropped out of the University of Pennsylvania and began buying commercial property after serving in the military during World War II.

Russell Simmons, multimillionaire cofounder of Def Jam Recordings, founder Russell Simmons Music Group, creator of Phat Farm and Baby Phat fashions, founding partner of UniRush Financial Services, creator of Global Grind website, best-selling author, movie and TV producer.

He left City College of New York at the age of twenty (after four years) to begin promoting local rap music acts (which he eventually signed to his music label) and producing records. He never graduated from college. There's a lot of money to be made in music, but then again, there's a lot of money to be made in almost everything, and none of it is easy. Russell Simmons did it the hard way—one buck at a time, and he has now amassed a fortune estimated to be worth about $325 million.

John Simplot, billionaire potato king. He dropped out of the eighth grade and left home at the age of fourteen. He sorted potatoes and raised hogs before saving enough money to buy his first potato field. He made his first million by the age of thirty.

Frank Sinatra, singer, Oscar Award–winning actor. He never finished high school. Sinatra sold more than 150 million records, won an Academy Award, and was a key figure in one of the most successful nightclub acts of all time. A lot of this might be attributed to his natural talent, but his gift for keeping his career going for decades after his heyday is what is impressive. He was a smart businessman.

Isaac Merrit Singer, sewing machine inventor, multimillionaire founder of Singer Industries. He dropped out of elementary school. Although not as popular as it once was, there was a day when every girl's dream was to own a Singer sewing machine.

Derek Silvers, founder of CD Baby and MuckWork, professional musician, entrepreneur. He attended Berklee College of Music for three years, but it's unclear whether he graduated (he's sparse with his online biographies).

Jim Skinner, CEO of McDonald's for eight years. He never graduated from college. It's not surprising since Ray Kroc, the founder, did not have a degree.

Alfred E. Smith, governor of New York and presidential candidate. He left school at the age of fourteen to help his family after his father died. He would later joke that he received his FFM degree from the Fulton Fish Market in New York City.

Dylan Smith, multimillionaire cofounder of Box.net. Dropped out of Duke University and headed to Silicon Valley to build the business.

Yet another founder/cofounder of a technology company, this time for data storage. It's not surprising. Cloud storage has become the new norm, and Dylan Smith, along with his partner and the founder of Dropbox, have led the way. Not a day goes by that I don't use Cloud storage.

Elinor Smith, aviatrix, the Flying Flapper. By the time she was seventeen, she was ferrying passengers on short hops from Roosevelt Field in Long Island. By eighteen, she had her own sight-seeing business. Never attended college.

O. Bruton Smith, billionaire. "I didn't attend college, but still had a good time. I think I probably had more fun than any human deserves a right to have." (Quote is from an article in *Forbes* in 2007)

Walter L. Smith, president of Florida A&M University. Dropped out of high school but later earned an equivalency diploma at the age of twenty-three.

Will Smith, Grammy Award–winning rapper, actor. He did not attend college. As the Fresh Prince, he and DJ Jazzy Jeff released their first album before he finished high school. They received the first Grammy awarded to a hip-hop act. Due to the success of that first album, Smith decided to forgo college for show business. Most people know Will for his portrayal of Captain Steve Hiller in *Independence Day* or Agent J in *Men in Black*, or numerous other roles. What you probably didn't know is that Will Smith is the only actor to have eight consecutive films gross over $100 million in the domestic box office, ten consecutive films gross over $150 million internationally, and that he is the only actor to have eight consecutive films in which he starred open at number one in the domestic box office tally. This is a heck of a feat for anyone, but for a kid who never went to college, it's even more impressive. At last count, he was estimated to be worth more than $200 million, an indication that he does more than collect a paycheck, though I'm sure his paychecks are substantial.

Daniel Snyder, billionaire owner of Snyder Communications and Red Zone Capital, owner of the Washington Redskins. He dropped out of the University of Maryland. He owns the Redskins, who were previously owned by Jack Kent Cooke, another member on this list. The Redskins have recently been valued at approximately $2.85 billion.

Josh Sommer, founder, Chordoma Foundation. Dropped out of Duke University to cofound the foundation to fund research on this rare bone cancer.

Bruce Springsteen, Grammy Award–winning and Oscar Award–winning singer and songwriter. He never attended college.

Sylvester Stallone, actor, director, and screenwriter. He struggled in high school and was expelled from several schools. He studied drama at the American College of Switzerland and the University of Miami, but he dropped out to pursue an acting career in New York City.

Not many people have managed to capture the hearts and minds of the American public, at least not in the way that Stallone has. He wrote the screenplay for, and starred in, *Rocky*, and wrote several other screenplays and starred in many other films, including six where he portrayed the same character (Rocky Balboa) and four where he portrayed John Rambo, of the *First Blood* and *Rambo* fame.

In *Rocky IV,* he was able to dig into the psyche of millions of Americans who were disgusted with the cold war, and he pitted Rocky against the Russians to elicit emotions we probably didn't even know we had.

Celebrity Net Worth estimates him to be worth about $400 million.

Jake Steinfeld, bodybuilder, founder of Body by Jake, cofounder of FitTV and Major League Lacrosse. Dropped out of the State University of New York and moved to California to follow his passion as a bodybuilder.

Jake has probably done more to help people get in shape than any MD I can think of. And he's probably made them feel better about themselves in the process.

Biz Stone, cofounder of Twitter and Obvious. A college dropout.

W. Clement Stone, multimillionaire insurance businessman, founder of *Success* magazine, and author of a number of books on a positive mental attitude. At the age of six, he sold newspapers on the south side of Chicago. By the age of thirteen, he owned his own newsstand. He continued to work odd jobs until his mother bought a small insurance agency, where he helped her by selling insurance. At the age of twenty-one, with $100 in his pocket, he established the Combined Registry Company insurance business, which he built into a multimillion-dollar business. He dropped out of elementary school but later attended high school night courses and some college.

Tom Stoppard, Tony Award–winning playwright and Oscar Award–winning screenwriter. He didn't like school, so he never attended college.

Quentin Tarantino, movie director, producer, and screenwriter. He was a high school dropout.

Benedikt Taschen, publisher of Taschen Books. At eighteen, he opened his first comic store. At nineteen, he founded Taschen Books, publisher of fine art books. As he noted, he saw no point in going to a university.

Alfred Taubman, billionaire chairman of Sotheby, real estate investor, mall operator. Dropped out of the University of Michigan. Made his first fortune investing in shopping malls. Pledged a donation of $56 million to the University of Michigan in 2012.

Jack Crawford Taylor, billionaire founder of Enterprise Rent-a-Car. Dropped out of Washington University to serve as a fighter pilot in the navy during World War II. Sold cars after the war before starting a car-leasing company. It's difficult to compete with Hertz and Avis, and yet Crawford not only competed, he succeeded. He hasn't put them out of business, but he sure has made a name for himself.

Zachary Taylor, US president, general. Little formal schooling. Homeschooled.

Dave Thomas, billionaire founder of Wendy's. As a youngster his family moved around a lot. While working as a busboy at the age of fifteen, he refused to move again. Instead, he dropped out of high school and went to work full-time at a restaurant (moving in with the family that owned the restaurant).

Tim Thornhill, owner, Mendocino Wine Company and green entrepreneur. He dropped out of high school after the ninth grade and started working on ranches near his hometown of Houston, Texas. He then moved to Orlando, FL., and later to California.

Kip Tindell, founder of the Container Store. Dropped out of the University of Texas. As he noted, "I crammed a four-year program into about eight years." (From the College Dropouts Hall of Fame) Isn't it ironic that the Container Store, founded by a college dropout, is the place almost everyone goes to shop for college-dorm storage?

Leo Tolstoy, count, novelist (*War and Peace, Anna Karenina*). Dropped out after three years at the university. Put him in the same category as Herman Melville, James Fenimore Cooper, J.D. Salinger, and F. Scott Fitzgerald, a non-degreed writer who wrote books that later became mandatory reading.

Lynsi Torres, billionaire owner of In-N-Out Burger (inherited). Did not attend college.

Harry Truman, US president. He was the last of the presidents who did not go to college. Truman had his share of tough decisions to make. He took office after the death of Roosevelt, while WWII was still raging. It was Truman who made the decision to drop the bombs on Hiroshima and Nagasaki, and it was Truman who presided over the country during the initial stages of the cold war. He is also credited with helping to found the United Nations and NATO. In addition, he issued the Truman Doctrine in 1947, and enacted the $13 billion Marshall Plan to help rebuild Western Europe.

Harriet Tubman, abolitionist, former slave, humanitarian, spy, nurse, suffragist. Did not attend college. Though illiterate herself, Tubman was not only a big promoter of education, she was a proponent of equal rights, and all of this during a time when it was difficult for a woman—let alone a former slave—to get things done. She was remarkable.

Frederick Tudor, the Ice King. Dropped out of school at the age of thirteen. After loafing around for a few years, he retired to his family's country estate to fish, farm, and hunt. Eventually he began shipping ice from his Massachusetts pond to tropical countries for use in cooling drinks and in making ice cream.

Albert Ueltschi, billionaire founder of FlightSafety International pilot training schools. Dropped out of the University of Kentucky to follow his passion—flying planes. After flying for PanAm for ten years, he founded FlightSafety. He is also enshrined in the Aviation Hall of Fame.

Leon Uris, best-selling novelist. Dropped out of high school at the age of seventeen to join the US Marines.

Jay Van Andel, billionaire cofounder of Amway (now Alticor). Served in the army after high school. Founded Amway along with his best friend, Richard DeVos. At one point in your life, you are bound to have been exposed to Amway, for good or bad. No matter which, you can thank Jay Van Andel or Richard DeVos, both of whom are on this list.

Martin Van Buren, US president. Little formal education. Began studying law at the age of fourteen while apprenticing at a law firm.

Cornelius Vanderbilt, railroad magnate and one of the wealthiest Americans of the mid–1800s. Had little formal schooling. Was considered uncouth and illiterate until he became too rich to ignore. Vanderbilt is best known for building the New York Central Railroad.

He was one of the wealthiest people in US history, and provided the initial gift to found Vanderbilt University. Calculating his wealth in today's dollars (as a percent of the GND), he would be ranked second or third, behind only John D. Rockefeller (1) and Andrew Carnegie (2 or 3), at an estimated net worth of $147 billion.

His son built the Biltmore House in N.C., and it stands today as the largest house in the US, at approximately 178,000 square feet.

Anton van Leeuwenhoek, microbiologist, microscope maker, discoverer of bacteria, blood cells, and sperm cells. He dropped out of high school.

Jesse "The Body" Ventura, wrestler, actor, Minnesota governor. He dropped out of North Hennepin Community College after one year. Ventura may go down in history as having appeared in the only movie to have featured two future US governors (he and Arnold Schwarzenegger).

Lynn Vincent, best-selling ghostwriter. She dropped out of college to join the navy. Later she left the military to write full-time. She had three books on the best-seller lists in the same week.

Theodore Waitt, multimillionaire founder of Gateway Computers. He dropped out of the University of Iowa one semester short of a degree to start Gateway with his older brother in 1985.

Scott Walker, governor of Wisconsin. He walked away from Marquette University just thirty-four credits short of a degree. He left to take a job.

DeWitt Wallace, founder and publisher of *Reader's Digest*, philanthropist. He dropped out of Macalester College in Saint Paul, Minnesota, after one year. He dropped out of the University of California at Berkeley after the second year. For many years, the *Reader's Digest* was not only the magazine to go to for TV schedules but for general reading as well. Millions counted on it to provide news and entertainment, and yet it was begun by a man who dropped out of college.

Y. C. Wang, billionaire founder of Formosa Plastics. He never attended high school.

Gertrude Chandler Warner, children's book author, *The Boxcar Children* series.

Ty Warner, billionaire developer of Beanie Babies, hotel owner, real estate investor. He dropped out of Kalamazoo College to work as a busboy, valet parker, bellman, and fruit vendor. Eventually he went on the road selling encyclopedias, cameras, and plush toys.

Dennis Washington, billionaire road contractor. The day after his high school graduation, he headed to Alaska to work in construction for two years. By the age of twenty-two, he was working for his uncle on his first interstate highway job. He now owns a copper mine in Montana, a barge business in Vancouver, and Montana Rail Link.

George Washington, US president, general, plantation owner. He ended his education after a few years of elementary school. The first president of the United States, and arguably, one of its best, Washington never even finished elementary school.

Sidney Weinberg, aka "Mr. Wall Street," managing partner of Goldman Sachs. Dropped out of the seventh grade in Brooklyn.

David Weinreb, CEO of Howard Hughes, TV commercial actor. He dropped out of New York University and wound up in Texas selling real estate.

Dean White, billionaire hotelier and billboard magnate. Dropped out of the University of Nebraska to join the Merchant Marine Academy. Served during World War II, then took over family business after the war and built it into a billboard and real estate empire.

Walt Whitman, poet, self-published. Elementary school dropout. Whitman is among the most influential poets in the American canon, often called the father of free verse.

He was both admired, respected, and cursed during his lifetime as his work was claimed to be "overtly sexual." And yet, to this day, teachers require children to study his works in literature. What they *don't* tell the children is that Whitman dropped out of elementary school.

Dan Wilks, billionaire founder of Wilks Masonry and Frac Tech. Did not attend college. Dan and Farris Wilks were brothers living in a small town about one hundred forty miles west of Dallas. They were the sons of a bricklayer, and they branched out from the family business to found Frac Tech, which designs, builds, and deploys the pumper rigs drillers use to blast open shale formations. They built that business into the third largest business of its kind in the country and sold it in 2011 for $3.2 billion.

Farris Wilks (brother of Dan Wilks), billionaire founder of Wilks Masonry and Frac Tech. Did not attend college.

Evan Williams, billionaire co-developer of Blogger, Twitter, and Medium, a social blogging platform. He dropped out of the University of Nebraska to write computer code.

Kemmons Wilson, multimillionaire founder of Holiday Inns. Dropped out of high school.

Anna Wintour, editor-in-chief, *Vogue* magazine. Did not attend college.

Jack Wong, CEO of Meizu (Chinese phone maker). He is a high school dropout and one-time factory worker.

Orville Wright, inventor of the airplane. Dropped out of high school in his junior year to open a printing business.

Wilbur Wright, (Orville's brother) inventor of the airplane. Completed four years of high school but never received his diploma. Did not attend college.

William Wrigley Jr., founder, Wrigley's chewing gum. Also owner of the Chicago Clubs, Wrigley Field, the Arizona Biltmore Hotel, and Catalina Island. Expelled from grammar school. Never attended high school or college.

Hiroshi Yamauchi, multimillionaire CEO of Nintendo. Dropped out of college.

Chaleo Yoovidhya, billionaire founder of Red Bull. He had little formal education, but he still founded a pharma business in the 1960s that developed into the Red Bull energy-drink business.

Wong Kwong Yu, billionaire founder of the Gome retail stores. He left school at the age of sixteen.

Emile Zola, French novelist. He failed his baccalaureate, which I believe is the French way of saying he did not graduate from college.

Dale Stephens, founder of Uncollege.org. Dropped out of Hendrix College for at least two years to launch Uncollege.org. He was funded $100,000 by Peter Thiel, cofounder of PayPal, via Thiel's college dropout project.

Below are quotes from a few of the people on our list:

"Eventually I came to conclude that I could not find real knowledge in academic life, only hierarchies of knowledge that led, ultimately, to more hierarchies, not to more knowledge. I began to see university learning as limited, human, and relative. What was seen as absolutely up-to-date did not consider the infinite and timeless."
—Sharon Daniels, author, *The World of Truth*

"Schools teach children to obey. They espouse the things we—the ruling generation—want kids to know. No wonder most schools are pressure cookers where bored teachers meet bored children. . . . Modern education is a wasted investment. It doesn't deliver what we need the most: creative answers to the challenges of our times. . . . It isn't a surprise that many of the people who've had the greatest influence on our times were—from the perspective of education—failures."

—Jurriaan Kamp, editor, *Ode* magazine

"There are only about 10 to 20 rappers that are in the game making money with album after album. Do the math and get your education." Obviously, Jay Z believes in education despite being on this list.

—Jay Z

"The things that have been most valuable to me I did not learn in school. Traditional education is based on facts and figures and passing tests—not on a comprehension of the material, and its application to your life. . . . I know how to learn anything I want to learn. . . . Give me the book, and I do not need somebody to stand up in front of the class.

—Will Smith, actor

Records

We've seen the individual accomplishments of these people, now consider what these things mean. Take a look at a few of the records that the people or companies they built hold.

The World's Best at a Glance

Most valuable company: Apple
Largest software company: Microsoft
Largest database company: Oracle
Largest computer hardware company: Dell
Largest social media company: Facebook
Largest messenger service company: What's App (now part of Facebook)
Largest content management system: Wordpress
Largest microblogging platform: Tumblr
Largest micro/microblogging platform: Twitter
Highest grossing movies of all time: James Cameron's *Titanic* and *Avatar*
Richest man in the world: Bill Gates, at approximately $87 billion
Second richest man in the world: Amancio Ortega Gaona, at about $75 billion
Most successful car manufacturer: Henry Ford, founder of Ford

Motor Company
Best-selling cookies: Mrs. Fields and Famous Amos
Most translated book: *The Alchemist*
Top consumer electronics company (US): Best Buy
First great American novel: *Huckleberry Finn*
America's greatest architect: Frank Lloyd Wright
Father of modern physics and of observational astronomy: Galileo
Most successful rap-music label: Russell Simmons (Def Jam Records)
One of the most influential men in history: Alexander Graham Bell
Most prolific inventor: Thomas Alva Edison
Largest transparently operated charitable foundation: Bill & Melinda Gates Foundation
Most intelligence man: Leonardo da Vinci
World's greatest sculptor: Michelangelo
Highest grossing actor: Will Smith
World's greatest chess player: Bobby Fischer

These are just a few of the records and accomplishments the "uneducated" can lay claim to. Suffice it to say, without the products, services, and businesses these people were responsible for, our lives would be drastically different. Take a moment to ponder it, and I'm sure you'll see that some facet of your daily life has been affected.

It's seldom you'll find the traits of success—optimism, perseverance, and realism—in one person, but there are ways to get around that. If a person has perseverance and optimism, and they're joined by someone with realism, then it can work. In fact, any combination of the three can work if given the chance.

Summary

So, do you *have* to go to college? Most people say so—your parents, teachers, most of the advice books and columns. "You'll never succeed without it," people say.

But what will happen if you don't? Maybe you'll be like John Doe (real person, but fake name), who lives in the apartments down the road. He lives a miserable life, blaming all of his woes on not having a chance in life because he doesn't have a degree. Or maybe you'll be like Vincenzo Attanasio (real person but fake name) who also never went to college. He lives down the street and he has three magnificent kids, a decent job, and a beautiful wife. They eat dinner together every night, play at the park every weekend, and enjoy each day of their lives. The whole family seems happy.

What more could you ask for?

Is Vincenzo happy because he *didn't* go to college? No.

Is John *unhappy* because he didn't go? No.

They are where they are because that's where they've put themselves. Read that last part again—that's where *they've* put themselves. Success or failure—the definition and the outcome—are up to you.

Bottom Line

We're slowly learning how to treat people in this country, but slowly is the key word. We need to get to the point where *everyone* and I mean *everyone* is treated the same, based on what they are able to do, no matter what color they are, no matter what religion they practice, no matter who they choose to sleep with, and no matter what the level of formal education is.

If you're working between two people and the one on your left is a better designer than the one on your right, does it matter if the person on the left has a college degree or not?

A Thought

Last night, I was preparing for sleep and I was reading a book. I happened to know that the author of that book was a non-degreed person. I thought about that, and realized that she was fortunate. For many occupations a degree is required. That made me ponder on what the world would be like if we did not have the accomplishments of non-degreed people.

The more I thought about it, the more I laughed. I was reading the book on iBooks (developed by Apple) and I was using an iPad to read it, also developed by Apple. The lightbulb which provided the light was originally invented by Thomas Edison, and even the electricity to run the lamp was an indirect result of Benjamin Franklin's work. That line of thinking made me wonder what else in our daily lives would be affected.

Where Would You
Be without Them?

If you take away the achievements of these non-degreed people, what are you left with?

Would the country be the same without the contributions of George Washington? Would anyone else besides Abe Lincoln have had the willpower and stamina to fight a civil war and free the slaves? And though not adored, who would have stepped up to run the county when Lincoln was shot? Andrew Johnson did, and without a degree. Would England still be an ally if Churchill hadn't led them through WWII? If Truman hadn't decided to drop the atomic bombs on Japan, would the next president? How would that have affected the world?

Would we have a phone without Alexander Graham Bell? A lightbulb without Edison or Tesla? How would electricity be different if Ben Franklin hadn't been around? And what about the automobile industry without Ford? Or the railroad business without Vanderbilt, the oil industry without Rockefeller, or the steel industry without Carnegie?

And how about buying or selling a car at AutoNation? Forget it. You couldn't ride your Segway or rent an Uber car to go to IKEA, because none of those companies would exist, at least not in their present form.

Reading is what many do at night to relax before bedtime. But don't think of reading Ernest Hemingway, Edgar Allan Poe, William Faulkner, Mark Twain, Jane Austen, George Orwell, and hundreds of others. You couldn't enjoy a science-fiction book by Ray Bradbury or a poem by Joseph Brodsky. None of them had degrees. You couldn't learn how to train your dog from Cesar Millan or read Moby Dick (even if you wanted to).

The next time you visit your parents, remember that you can't take a picture with their Polaroid or Kodak cameras—and they probably still have them. And don't plan on pulling out your Blackberry phone (if you still own one) from your Polo shirt, as neither would be there. You couldn't shop at Virgin Records or fly to London on Virgin Atlantic Airways.

By the way, that trip you're taking—don't fly. Neither Wilbur or Orville Wright (inventors of the airplane) had degrees. And if you're going to Chicago, don't chew Wrigley's gum, or plan on watching a Cubs game, or even going to Wrigley Field, as William Wrigley was expelled from grammar school.

Oh, and don't plan on playing Nintendo while on vacation, either (or any other time, for that matter). And don't think of listening to iTunes as you relax. Not only was iTunes developed by Apple, it may have been inspired by Napster and Napster's non-degreed founders.

If you plan to play Minecraft while staring at a Picasso, think again. Minecraft was developed by a non-degreed person (Persson), and Picasso was a non-degreed person.

Oh, and don't try stopping at Best Buy for a new DVD or anything else. It was founded by Richard Schulze, who is now a billionaire, though he probably doesn't care that he has no degree. And speaking of games, where would chess be without Bobby Fischer? Remember Bobby Fischer, who most consider the greatest chess player in the world?

Don't think of shopping at Christie's auctions for some Gucci items and then flying with your Samsonite luggage to a discount Puma store. You wouldn't be able to do any of that without François Pinault. And Prada and Ralph Lauren wouldn't show up the fashion shows in Milan.

You say you're hungry? On your way home from work you couldn't stop at Kroger or Whole Foods to get dinner, or even pick up a meal at McDonald's or Wendy's—their founders are non-degreed.

And you wouldn't be able to eat Mrs. Fields or Famous Amos cookies at the mall, or eat an Auntie Anne's pretzel. And if you do eat too many cookies and you're thinking of going on a diet, don't plan on drinking Slim Fast. It isn't there.

You couldn't marvel at the flavor of Carvel ice cream while pondering new legislation by Julia Carson, James Byrnes, John Glenn, or Robert Byrd—or reading about it on Mashable. And you couldn't relax and enjoy an Irving Berlin film, or listen to music by Tony Bennet, or watch a film with Halle Berry. In fact, don't think about watching anything on Fox or eating Dole fruit. They were both founded by non-degreed people.

You won't be able to spend the night or gamble at the Golden Nugget

Casino or eat at Landry's, Morton's, or the Rainforest Cafe, or any other of the five hundred restaurants owned by Tilman Fertitta.

Without non-degreed people, you wouldn't be listening to songs by Madonna, Jay Z, P. Diddy, J. Lo, and many others. You couldn't even listen to Mozart. And whose romantic songs would you listen to with your sweetheart on a moonlit night? Not Dean Martin's or Frank Sinatra's.

Marcus Loew founded the Loew's movie theaters. Where else would you go to see movies? Would everyone be at AMC? Would the chain be the same? And if he hadn't cofounded MGM, would it be the same? Would it even exist? How about United Artists?

It would be impossible to rally behind a Charles Bronson film or drool over Gisele Bündchen (as I know many of you do), or be entertained by a movie directed by James Cameron or one starring James Cagney or Michael Caine or Leonardo DiCaprio. And by the way, you can't take your kids to see a Disney movie or go to Disneyland, or watch The Simpsons, reruns of Cheers, or any Clint Eastwood movie.

We would have no Jaws or ET or many other movies to remember (Terminator, Aliens, Saving Private Ryan, Avatar, Titanic). And you couldn't watch movies with Sylvester Stallone. Robert De Niro, Tom Hanks, Sofia Loren (Sofia Scicolone), and dozens more.

What would the Brooklyn Nets be like without Jay Z? Or the Miami Heat without Micky Arison? Or the Dolphins without Huizenga? Or the San Diego Padres without the previous ownership of Ray Kroc? Or the Ravens or Browns without Art Modell? Or the New York

Rangers or the New York Knicks without Charles Dolan? Jack Kent Cooke was the former owner of the Washington Redskins (NFL), the Los Angeles Lakers (NBA), the Los Angeles Kings (NHL), and the Los Angeles Wolves (United Soccer Association). You get my point.

And you couldn't see a fight at Madison Square Garden, or watch Game of Thrones, or anything else, on HBO. And if you're looking for a jog after dinner, remember, you can't wear Reebok shoes.

And for good or bad, how about the Bank of America?

And how would your house get cleaned without an Oreck? Who hasn't vacuumed with an Oreck? If you haven't, you should, and if you have, you know what I mean.

And don't try to Tweet your spouse that you're not coming home on time. Remember, there is no iPhone and no Twitter. And by the way, on your next business trip, don't consider renting an Enterprise car. Figure out an alternative. And don't plan on staying at a Holiday Inn or reading Vogue magazine while there. Or driving anything that uses Firestone tires or Discount tires. And while you're driving on some other company's tires, don't think of trying to find songs by The Supremes, The Temptations, Smokey Robinson and the Miracles, Marvin Gaye, or any other of the hundreds of acts produced by Motown. Berry Gordy was non-degreed.

You wouldn't have much in the way of computers without Bill Gates's operating system, which powers most of the world's PCs, or Jobs's and Wozniak's hardware and software, which power your Mac.

And what about Michael Dell? His company is one of the largest manufacturers of hardware for PCs; even Hewlett-Packard uses Microsoft for its computers. And where would you be without Word and Excel and PowerPoint? Or Pages or Numbers or Keynote? You couldn't take notes on Evernote, store them on Dropbox or Boxnet, or listen to Rush Limbaugh or Sean Hannity on your way home from work.

And if the sun's glare is bothering you while you drive, don't reach for a pair of sunglasses by Ray-Ban, Oakley, Vogue Eyewear, Persol, Oliver Peoples or Alain Mikli. And if you want to take your loved one to a concert, you can't use Ticketmaster.

The next time you plug into your USB hub or wireless router or type on your iPad keyboard, think of Chet Pipkin, the billionaire founder of Belkin. You would have to rely on someone else if not for him. And you couldn't apply for a loan at Lending Tree or go to Ask.com or Match.com on the Internet.

About 74 million websites run on Wordpress. Who would you use to host yours? Could you still send your siblings or favorite vendors money through PayPal? What would the other company look like? More than a billion people couldn't share their lives on Facebook, Twitter, or Tumblr, and hundreds of millions more wouldn't have Oracle software to conduct their business with.

So the next time you're tempted to disparage someone who doesn't hold a university degree, think of what you'd be missing without those people. The above is but a small sampling of the many achievements the people on our lists have created with the companies they built. Multiply that by a factor of ten and you are likely closer to the truth.

Before closing, I'd like you to consider this:

According to an article by *The NY Times* in 2015, and to the book, *Facts About the Presidents,* twelve presidents did not graduate from college, including:

- George Washington
- James Monroe
- Andrew Jackson
- Martin Van Buren
- William Henry Harrison
- Zachary Taylor
- Millard Fillmore
- Abraham Lincoln
- Andrew Johnson
- Grover Cleveland
- William McKinley
- Harry S. Truman

That's twelve presidents without degrees—25 percent of them. Obama is the forty-fourth president, although Grover Cleveland served twice, which means that only forty-three different people have been president. To put that in perspective, that's one in four presidents who did not have a degree. And eight of those never went to college. (According to an article in the Washington Post on February 15, 2015)

In Closing

When we look at this list as individuals, we see people who achieved something great despite the odds, but when we analyze it as a whole, we see something else. We see people in almost *every* field who *dominate* the list, and in every case, they had no degree.

Take a look for yourself:

Steve Jobs
Bill Gates
Mark Zuckerberg
Larry Ellison
Michael Dell

These are the men who ran the three biggest computer technology companies, the two biggest software companies, and two of the biggest social media companies, not to mention that Facebook bought WhatsApp for $19B and Microsoft purchased LinkedIn for $26B.

We can then move on to entertainment and fashion.

Steven Spielberg
Robert De Niro

Madonna

Jay Z

P. Diddy

J. Lo

Ralph Lauren

Mention these names to one hundred people, and ninety-nine of them will probably recognize them. I doubt that would happen with other names. These are people who have made their mark on society. They've done it in a big way, and they've done it *without* the benefit of a degree.

Would they have been just as successful *with* a degree? Who knows? But the mere fact that we're asking such a question is significant. Would Steve Jobs still have founded Apple had he stayed at Reed College? Would Mark Zuckerberg have started Facebook had he remained at Harvard?

I don't know the answer, but the significance lies in the fact that Jobs *didn't* stay at Reed and Zuckerberg *didn't* finish his degree at Harvard, and yet both still made it beyond anyone's wildest expectations.

One more thing we ought to mention: we have discussed the exceptions, the rare exceptions, to the rule—those hell-bent on succeeding.

What about the millions of "normal" people who didn't go to college and who don't necessarily want to succeed in the same way? Those who measure success differently? Suppose success means a steady job, a good marriage, and a happy and healthy family?

If that is your definition of success, you're in luck, as it's easily attainable. It basically takes three things:

1. Figure out what you want.
2. Find a soul mate who wants the same thing.
3. Let your kids and spouse know you love them.

My nephew and youngest son have beautiful houses, great jobs, magnificent wives, and spectacular kids. They're always happy and in a good mood, and—you guessed it—neither one has a degree. Neither one of them is a billionaire, but who cares? They have what's important in life.

Sounds simple, I know. But I've been living that life for more than forty-seven years, and I'm one of the happiest guys you'll know. In fact, I've been married to my wife for forty-seven years (since we were seventeen) and we're both still in love. And in case you're wondering—no, I don't have a college degree. I never even finished high school.

Other Books Coming Soon

Fiction

A Promise of Vengeance (Fantasy)
My first fantasy, and the first book in a four-book series—the Rules of Vengeance. (Three are already written and the fourth is being outlined.)

Murder Is Invisible ### (going through editing)
Frankie and Nicky are back.

Non-Fiction

- No Mistakes Grammar, Volume I, Misused Words. (being proofread)
- No Mistakes Grammar, Volume II, Misused Words for Business (being proofread)
- No Mistakes Grammar, Volume III, More Misused Words. (being proofread)
- No Mistakes Writing, Writing Shortcuts (being proofread)
- Uneducated—Thirty-Seven People Who Redefined the Definition of Education (being proofread)
- Whiskers and Bear—Volume I of the Life on the Farm Series (sent to editor)

Children's Books

- No Mistakes Grammar for Kids, Volume I—Much and Many (Sent to editor)
- No Mistakes Grammar for Kids, Volume II—Lie and Lay (Sent to editor)
- No Mistakes Grammar for Kids, Volume III—Then and Than (Sent to editor)
- Shinobi Goes to School—Life on the Farm for kids. (working on illustrations)

Get on the mailing list and you'll be sure to be notified of release dates and sales. Mailing list

Acknowledgments

As usual, there are too many people to thank and not enough room to thank them, so I'll make this short and sweet. Heartfelt thanks to my mother and father. They're no longer with me in the physical world, but they're always with me.

Giacomo

About the Author

Giacomo Giammatteo is the author of gritty crime dramas about murder, mystery, and family. He also writes non-fiction books including the No Mistakes Careers series.

When Giacomo isn't writing, he's helping his wife take care of the animals on their sanctuary. At last count they had 45 animals—11 dogs, a horse, 6 cats, and 26 pigs.

Oh, and one crazy—and very large—wild boar, who takes walks with Giacomo every day and happens to also be his best buddy.

www.ingramcontent.com/pod-product-compliance
Lightning Source LLC
Chambersburg PA
CBHW051730020426
42333CB00014B/1248